Ashley Jackson's Yorkshire Moors

Winter Solitude

Ashley Jackson's Yorkshire Moors

A LOVE AFFAIR

First published in Great Britain 2000
Dalesman Publishing Company Limited
Stable Courtyard
Broughton Hall
Skipton
North Yorkshire BD23 3AZ

Text © Ashley Jackson

A British Library Cataloguing in Publication record
is available for this book

ISBN 1 85568 180 3
Designed by Jonathan Newdick
Typeset by SPAN Graphics Limited
Colour Origination by Grasmere Digital Imaging Limited
Printed by Midas Printing (HK) Limited

Thanks

To Heather, my daughter and manager, for working and helping me
to fulfil as an artist, one of my dreams – this book – a dream on which
I have worked long and hard, and have at last been able to see come to
life.
To Robert Flanagan, general manager of Dalesman Publishing
Company, for having faith in me and my work. And my final thanks to
the county of Yorkshire and its people for lighting within me my
passion to capture in all her glory, God's Own County, the Texas of
England.

Contents

Dedication

To Anne, my wife, for all her love, help and understanding in living with an artist of mind, soul and temperament. For staying with me through all the lean years and, most of all, for having faith in me; when critics doubted, she encouraged. I shall be eternally grateful.

Foreword by Sir Bernard Ingham

Familiarity breeds contempt, they say. Ashley Jackson proves otherwise. This book is the product of a 50-year love affair with the wilder, millstone grittier bits of my native Yorkshire. The moors are his mistress, he confesses, and he reveals her in her many moods. They are mostly bleak as distinct from foul – wind-blown, cloud-hung, mist-shrouded, rain-lashed, on fire and snow-bound. He is also partial to remote homesteads such as the one his daughter lives in, and he captures them complete with their telephone or electricity poles. He is "the patron saint of telegraph poles", according to a friend. But then Ashley paints things as they are and not for the sentimentalists, though he's not above a bit of artistic licence or straying into Wharfedale and Swaledale any more than I am. I reckon we are both entitled to a certain indulgence after worshipping the same mistress for half a century. The difference is that, whereas I have mostly delighted in her these last 35 years from the distance of the metropolis and Surrey, Ashley embraces her daily. And he paints her as nature intended and as the spirit moves him.

Indeed, I get the impression that walking with Ashley is as frustrating an experience as is hiking with my son. He is liable to set up shop, as it were, as the scene takes him just as my ornithologist John stops, starts, loiters and is overcome with a suppressed ecstasy as he captures a bird in his binoculars. They are better walking alone because for them in their different ways the wild is an intensely personal and emotional experience. Consequently, I have not been privileged to see him at "work", though he keeps threatening to teach me how to paint for the benefit of TV viewers. Instead, my encounters with him have been socio-commercial: as guests of Owen O'Neill, late of British Gas, at a Headingley Test match; opening his "Earth, Wind and Fire" exhibition in the Lowry Museum in Salford; and at the launch of my "Yorkshire Millennium" book in York. With peculiar insight, he seems to have divined me as a moors man from the first. His generosity has made me the proud owner of two of his dripping, moor-drizzle-cloud layered paintings of the Pennines above his studio in Holmfirth which the director of TV's "Last of the Summer Wine" somehow always manages to bathe in sunshine.

My Pennine moors are a plateau or two further north above Calderdale, which Ashley captures on Blackshaw Edge near my native Hebden Bridge where he had a surreal encounter with a prophetic gypsy woman bearing a gift of goose eggs. I was born to them, to the Brontës' inspiration. I tramped them endlessly, glorying in their solitude, their desolation and the run of the ranges of hills into a purpling distance. Ashley came to them via the tragedy of Penang, Scotland and Barnsley which nurtured his talent. You will come to understand why we – him and me – think the world of her, the mistress who always beckons.

Give me the arts, for art is beauty.
Beauty is also in a woman.
But when I stand upon these moors
I see a beauty that never dies
As time comes and goes.
But woman's beauty fades with time.
And equal to beauty is companionship. Which woman has.
Funny, with both these gifts one cannot touch them.
Which is beauty in itself.

ASHLEY JACKSON 1967

Introduction

The passion and intensity that prompted the words on the facing page more than 30 years ago still burns deeply today. My art, my moors and my own woman, Anne – my wife of 38 years, mother of my two daughters and grandmother to four – have provided me with the essence of life. They remain my purpose for breathing, and to these three I will be eternally grateful. I once wrote: "Years go by as fast as cat's eyes on a motorway. The art of living is to make use of what you've got and use it to the full. Most people do not know what they are living for. But once you have found out, you have the jewel of life." I count myself fortunate to possess that jewel: a career that takes me out into the open to enjoy all that we have been freely granted: the skies, the moors, the valleys, the beautiful trees – nature's playground, which I call "the great cathedral of the open air". To walk it, let alone paint it, is a privilege that has been bestowed upon me, which I will never take for granted. To capture the landscapes and seascapes of the earth, and more particularly, Yorkshire, has been my vocation ever since I was nine years of age. I look upon it as a calling, and as so, treat it with the reverence it deserves. I have striven to portray every mood of nature as she takes on her fight against all that the elements throw at her, whether that be rain, wind, snow or fire.

My fascination for Yorkshire, my love affair with God's own county, where the moors seem to penetrate the very skies, goes back to 1950 and a terraced house in Huddersfield, my first home in England. It was from here that the brooding majesty of the Pennines took a grip on my life that was never to falter. These were to become more than merely moors and hills; in time they became my inspiration, my saving grace. My early years had been unsettled, sometimes difficult, but now no longer did I feel like a cork bobbing in an empty sea, at the whim of tide or current. I began to detect a sense of direction. For this I owe a debt of gratitude to my step uncle, Malcolm, who was a year older than me. I had led a sheltered and privileged life at a Jesuit boarding school; he was to introduce me to a thrill of freedom I had never before experienced.

It was he who first took me up on to the wild, liberating moors. I still recall vividly my first dramatic glimpse of the panorama of the Colne Valley with its soot-blackened mills and industrial towns like Golcar and Slaithwaite. As I stood high on the Pennine tops I was filled with awe and wonder. That overwhelming surge of freedom also told me that I had at last found a home. The moors seemed to call to me, making me feel safe and secure. Suddenly, the fear and loneliness I had felt since arriving in Huddersfield evaporated. The moors brought strength and solace, enabling me to forget that I had lost a father. They eased the parting from my beloved grandpa, whom I missed terribly since he waved me goodbye in Penang harbour. They made me forget my back-to-back home in Milnsbridge, with its outside toilet and dustbins at the front

Teluk Bahang, Penang

door – a far cry from the colonial privilege I had known. I yielded to the beauty of the moors – Bradshaw, Cartworth, Holme Moss, Saddleworth, Wessenden – and, even as a young boy, I allowed myself to become at one with them.

And so these Yorkshire uplands ensnared me, becoming my life, my obsession, my mistress. They will always provoke in me deep passion. I am still surprised and troubled when I am asked if I get bored painting moorland scenes. People will ask: "Why not paint something else?" It is like asking a man who has been happily married to the same woman for 30 years if it's not boring and time for a change!

There is, as they fail to see, something about the Yorkshire moors that sets them apart from other moorland landscapes. Perhaps it is because I feel that I can communicate with hills, trees, grass and sky; understand their moods. I admire and respect them most when one moment they revel in their summer glory under bright sunshine, only abruptly to change mood as a soft rain falls adding sparkle to the landscape; when drystone walls reflect like broken mirrors on the scene. Even when crying, the Yorkshire Moors are beautiful. I have devoted all my life to experiencing, witnessing and capturing in water-colour the nuances in temperament of these moorland uplands, trying to fathom their depths. Although I have been married for nearly 40 years, I still do not profess to know every aspect of my wife, Anne; she still can surprise me. And, just like a

Woman on Bike. Teluk Bahang, Penang

woman, the moors have many different facets. I still have not viewed them all, nor, I am afraid to say, ever will.

To view Yorkshire in her 'wild mood' is an experience out of this world. My paintings often depict the rain, the mist and the wind, elements that have helped shape the character of the county and its people. To try to capture its wild and mysterious beauty, I love to venture on to the hills when it is raining – no matter whether it is starting, finishing or in full torrent – yet I never go with the sole intent of looking for a picture to paint. My aim is to walk, observe, listen to nature – and respond. I desire to know her intimately; to try to force out a painting would be wrong. It must be a mutual contract; she deserves this respect.

Whenever I begin a painting I become at one with my surroundings, absorbed by their all-consuming beauty. I try to freeze in watercolour that instant when the hairs on the back of my hands rise as I become captivated by the compelling power of the landscape. I embrace the solitude that I feel as I stand alone on the moor, savouring the emotion, willing this moment to last forever, for solitude is wholly different from loneliness. I prefer to be alone on my moor, choosing not to share it with anyone as I bask in its aura. To some this may appear selfish, but when I am painting alone, with no one to disturb or share with me the second great love of my life, I enjoy every moment of the intoxicating atmosphere. Then, and

The Road to the Isles

only then, am I able truly to paint, recording on paper the essence of the moors for others to see and appreciate. Only alone, can I put my whole soul into my work.

I have tried all my life to capture Yorkshire in her true glory, and capture her dignity in paintings, not pictures. A picture is mechanically constructed, anyone can create a picture. I have no desire merely to record a scene; my whole ambition in life has been to produce paintings, for they hold within them the essence and soul of the artist. How did I become so fascinated, so besotted, selfish and jealous of this awe-inspiring county, Yorkshire? Why did it take such a hold on me, when the first nine years of my life were spent in the Far East, where tall trees and long, hot, humid, sunny, predictable days were all I knew? As my life unfolds over the next pages, I will try to provide an insight into what gave me the strength and determination to become an artist and how I have endeavoured to capture with my brush the sort of grit that the Brontës depicted with their pens and that made me a man who is proud to call himself Ashley Jackson, Yorkshire Artist.

I emerged into a troubled world at the American Hospital, Penang, on October 22 1940, the son of Norman Valentine Jackson, general manager of the Tiger Beer Company, Singapore, and his young wife Dulcie Olga Scott (the daughter of a Scottish army bandleader and his Portuguese wife, who had retired to Penang). Despite the war raging in Europe, I passed my first months of life in the genteel and gracious world of colonial living. Singapore felt secure against invasion, until, as we now know, the Imperial Army swarmed over the impenetrable jungle and strolled in through the city's defenceless backdoor. Luckily, my father had the foresight to anticipate Japanese intentions.

He put his wife, mother and mother-in-law, along with me, now ten months, onto a crowded ship bound for India. My mother remembers vividly how the bombs of the Japanese army fell all around as we sailed out of the harbour. Singapore swiftly fell and my father became a prisoner of war at the infamous Changai Prison. Meanwhile, we were moved all around India; from Delhi to Bombay, to Agra into Karachi. Unbeknown to us, my father attempted to escape and was sent to a special camp in Borneo, an oriental Colditz. Some four years later, while the Australian troops advanced – and I celebrated my fifth birthday party with a bear charmer for an entertainer – my father was given a shovel and made to dig his own grave. At five, I lost the father that I had never got to know; my mother and grandmother were devastated.

Grandmother moved back to Limerick and life for my young, widowed mother and me looked very bleak. As my grandfather was Scottish by birth, we went from India to a place called Bridge of Weir in Paisley, Scotland. It was an army camp where we became war refugees, quartered with others in

Isle of Skye

draughty Nissen huts. Not all, however, was bleak. It was the first time my eyes had caught sight of the mist and strong, evocative light of the Northern hemisphere.

I can recollect visiting Loch Lomond and viewing, without the intrusion from giant trees, the huge expanse and spectacular vista before me. It was, in fact, Scotland not Yorkshire that awakened the urge to create pictures. It was here that school books became sketch pads as I played truant from the misery of the classroom, escaping into my own world, where momentarily I could forget the war, the father that I had lost, and my life. Here I could submerge myself in art, capturing the blue mountains and the vast canopy of sky. I owe Scotland a great debt for introducing me to my love of painting.

With the war over, we returned to Penang and our colonial life of servants and fine living. We lived with Grandpa Scott who was not only a musician but also an amateur artist and eccentric. He had erected in his garden a marquee decorated inside to represent the front parlour of an Englishman's home. Here he painted, and I watched in fascination and awe. My grandmother on my father's side, Dolores Jackson, was also an artist – and, in her maiden years, a flamenco dancer who danced for Queen Victoria.

Both sides of my family showed artistic talent and it is from them I inherited my sensitivity, appreciation of the arts and gift of painting. School, though, continued to be a problem for,

My studio/gallery in Dodworth

lacking a father, and despite teachers' attempts to improve my poor academic standard, I became – I am told – a spoilt brat of the worst kind. As my mother began to form a relationship with a British serviceman, Hedley Haigh, I was sent to a Jesuit boarding school. Again though, only in art did I excel. I found the whole experience hellish. I was so unhappy that my mother moved me to a day school in Kuala Lumpur where, despite being the only European in the class, I still came bottom! My mother informs me that even at this early stage, I had begun to develop an ability to talk my way out of trouble. My aptitude for art and conversation prevented me from being written off academically – and would continue to stand me in good stead.

My mother married Hedley, and the three of us boarded the P&O Liner, SS Canton, to England. As I glimpsed my second sighting of Britain on a foggy June morning, the white cliffs of Dover could, disappointingly, only faintly be made out. A pleasure boat sailed by the side of the ship and I heard the sounds of an accordion playing the Harry Lime theme, while men and women stood in their trench coats and trilbies to keep the mizzle away. These images have remained so real that if I close my eyes I can still feel the stark chill of that day and recapture a young boy's fear and apprehension. This was to be the beginning of my new life, a far cry from the one I had left behind.

Although Huddersfield had awakened me to the beauty of my natural surroundings and given me hope for the future, it

Glen Coe, Scotland

My gallery in Barnsley

wasn't until we moved to Barnsley that I could begin to put down roots. I had been without a true home for more than ten years and it was to provide me with the space and time to settle down. It was here, also, that my artistic and academic career began to flourish. A new confidence developed at my Catholic School, Holyrood, under the influence of the headmaster Mr Livesey, my art teacher Miss Netherwood, and form mistress Gertrude Young, all of whom showed faith in me. It was at school that I won first prize in an art competition (for road safety) and became a prefect and head boy. I left in December 1955, and it was Mr Livesey who arranged an appointment for me with the principal of Barnsley School of Art, Mr Harry Glover, to whom he had presented a folder of my artwork – collected, unbeknown to me, by Miss Netherwood in anticipation of that very day. I was admitted into the school on the strength of my portfolio alone, without having to take an entrance exam. My artwork had opened a door which, under normal circumstances, would have remained closed. Exams never were my forte!

At 16 I felt I could no longer expect my stepfather to continue to support me. I needed a wage and was taken on by a local painting and decorating company, continuing at school part-time. I vividly remember the day that was to prove a turning point in my life. I was working on a council estate at Worsbrough, cleaning the guttering of a house and emptying dirt

into a bucket when, from an open window, floated the voice of Doris Day singing *Que sera – what ever will be, will be...* The words struck me to the core. Was this to be it? Was I to be cleaning gutters for the rest of my life? I may have been at the top of a ladder – but I had hit rock bottom. God was on my side, though. The company folded three months later and I returned full-time to art school.

At 17 I took up a full-time apprenticeship with a remarkable man, Ron Darwent, a much admired signwriter and commercial artist. He taught me much more than the skill of signwriting; he taught me about life and became a much-loved father figure, taking over from Malcolm in helping me appreciate the moors. On evenings and weekends he would take me out and, as an experienced mountaineer and climber, taught me not only how to be at one with the moors – to climb and walk – but, most of all, to respect them. To this day, some 43 years on, I still indulge in a day's walking with Ron, the man who showed me truly how to love and appreciate the temperament of the moors. At 18 I met and fell in love with Anne, the woman who was to be my wife and who would have the most influence on, and confidence in, me as an artist.

She was, and still is, the only person who sees me cry, for I have always said: "The rain will wet you, the sun will burn you, the wind will chill you, but, only people will make you cry." She was the one who gave me the confidence to go out and achieve all that, physically, I could. As newly-weds in a two-up, two-down, rented terrace with outside toilet, me signwriting by day, it was she who knew how much I desired to give my life to painting. She persuaded me to allow her to support me in fulfilling my dream. She had total and absolute faith in me. Whenever I hear Kipling's poem, *If – If you can make one heap of all your winnings/ And risk it on one turn of pitch-and-toss/ And lose, and start again at your beginnings/ And never breathe a word about your loss* – I am reminded of the young, beautiful woman I married. For it is because of Anne that I can sit here writing the introduction to this book: my collection of love letters, my record of my everlasting affair that I have had with the moorland uplands of Yorkshire – my silent, all-embracing, all-demanding, tempestuous mistress.

As an artist approaching his sixtieth year, I could not have asked for any more in my journey of life. Yet, my greatest reward exists not on paper, but in the faces of my grandchildren. They are the greatest mark I have made on this earth. Many of my friends were called away before they were granted this privilege. And the very transience of life – like the fast-shifting moods of the moors – is why I have never dared take it for granted. To paint, and to be given this gift, makes me a lucky person indeed.

The collection

To see this spirit of Yorkshire
And its moors, through my eyes
Is one thing.
Many people look, but only
A few see
And feel its very soul.
For out of the monochrome mist,
You will feel the movement of
The moor.
It is the moors to me that makes
Life,
Makes life interesting and important.
I know of no substitute, to paint
With the heart and most of all the soul,
The beauty and force it possesses.

ASHLEY JACKSON SKETCHBOOK 1990

I

Dawns a new day – moorland odyssey 2001

The inspiration for this came on the day that I read the final chapter of George Orwell's rivetting *1984*, a novel I had been meaning to read for years. On completing it, I realised that many of its predictions – like the omnipresent Big Brother – were already with us. The book stirred and disturbed my imagination and I felt the need to drive up to Saddleworth Moor and stand upon ground that I knew was a timeless, secure and untouched stretch of moorland beauty. It was up here that I could reassure myself that not everything had changed, and suddenly I felt calmer and more confident about the future. As I looked on this spectacular vista, I hoped that this scene would look precisely the same in 2001. I was anxious to freeze this moment to give the impression that this piece of land, lying across the Yorkshire-Lancashire boundary, could in fact be anywhere in the universe, hence the subtitle for the painting. I feel that, of all my works, it comes closest to touching the soul of the landscape; closest to portraying the moor in all its colour and detail without being too clinically detailed. I wrote these words by my sketches of the work:

Colours are important; they put life into the landscape, giving it depth so that the eye will react. The landscape is trying to say something; this is her love letter. I believe if we could all read what she is trying to say we would look after her much more. We don't own her. She is there all the time – it is us who only stay a while – no man should own a mountain. We are only keepers of this earth; it is not ours but for the next of ours, in life, to follow.

I wanted to capture the light and shadows in the distant moor as they raced across my vision. More importantly, I wanted to capture this scene for the children of the Millennium. I dare not believe that moorland so beautiful as this could ever be despoiled by man or technology. I wanted to give the whole aura of the painting a caring character; I wanted it to say: "We need not fear the future, it can, if we want it, remain beautiful, we just need to preserve it as an inheritance for our future generations and think before we act; after all… dawn's a new day."

2

Above Wessenden

Whenever I gaze at this painting I want to stretch out my arms as far as my finger tips will allow, as though they are the wings of a bird, swooping over the valleys, gullies, lakes and peaks and into the far distant hills which weave together in harmony with the mist in the valleys, giving the illusion of islands shrouded in mist. This painting portrays to me all that I think of Yorkshire, her grandeur, strength, unassuming beauty – and her pride. I call her the Texas of England. Wessenden rates as one of my favourite moors. Many an hour I have passed, walking this tussocky landscape above the Holme Valley, two miles from Holmfirth on the A635, an unspoilt part of the Pennine chain. The rain had fallen earlier that day, clearing the air and providing me with an unbelievable vista. Not only did I want to capture the range before me, I wanted to illustrate the wonderful watersheds that nature had provided. I desperately wanted to convey the pattern of the sponges, the gullies and the becks which were chiselling out the wonderful shape and tone of the moor. In the far distance I could hear a skylark. As I frantically tried to emulate the reflection of colour and movement of clouds chasing across my vista, as though racing for shelter before the next storm broke, I was aware that a shadow crept over the moor. It would not be long before the next rain fell. But time waits for no man and it would not be too long before the bracken turned to a glowing burnt amber and my glistening, pure moor would take on another fascinating persona.

Words from Omar Khayyám's Rubaiyat echoed in my mind:

Dreaming when Dawn's left hand was in the sky
I heard a voice within the tavern cry
'Awake my little ones,
And fill the cup
Before life's liquor in its cup be dry'.

3

Low clouds – Gordale Scar

Painters, poets and writers have been drawn to the majesty of Gordale Scar. Some of the great Masters – Turner included – have been inspired and absorbed by the beauty of this limestone crown, set high in the Dales. In 1988 I chose to capture in watercolour my own vision. At first sight it was not, I am now ashamed to admit, the exhilarating experience I had envisioned: I had imagined it would be far grander and momentous. My predecessors had portrayed it in towering beauty – but to eyes accustomed to the sweep and enormity of the moors, they seemed merely to have exaggerated its height and width. Surely all of these Masters could not have been wrong? As I began to ponder over what it was about the Scar that could have motivated so many artists, a halo of light fell through a gap in the sky. It appeared to be leading me into the canyon. I knew then that I, too, had been seduced by its beguiling glory.

As the gorge's limestone shoulders overshadowed me; as the light threw down its spotlight onto the sheep grazing in the ravine's lush pasture, I instinctively understood why it had exerted so potent an influence on my predecessors. I suddenly felt squeezed of all my energies, like a nut in a vice, and reduced to shame for momentarily distrusting the magic of this Scar. Having been drawn into submission, I committed myself there and then to capture and portray her with the true reverence and respect that, beyond a question of a doubt, she deserved. Transfixed, and with all my energies focussed on to my paper, I began to paint. I was craving to capture this vision of beauty; her spiritual light enticing and beguiling me inwards, reflecting the sheer unadulterated soul of the gorge. While ensnared, words that I wrote some 20 years earlier sprang to my mind, giving me added determination to capture this place: *One must never give up. To be a painter is easy; to be an artist is a great gift. A painter just paints pictures, but an artist gives his soul.* I dedicate this work not only to a very fine goddess, Gordale Scar, whom I hope I have not disappointed, but to all those artists who have been allured and spellbound by the soul of this place. I am sorry that I ever doubted you.

4

At peace on the moor

I was driven to paint this work by a huge window that appeared in the sky and hung over the moor like a mirror image – it was spell binding. I felt as though I was being drawn into it, to reach beyond the world of clouds to the very spirit of nature. This is one of my most intense spiritual paintings; I was at one with the moor and my innermost feelings. I wrote at the side of this work:

I have always tried to paint what brings me
To the peace of landscape
And makes me fall in love with her.
I try to paint her soul,
And I've been trying to do so all my life.

At peace on the moor is truly a painting captured with my heart, hand and soul.

5

Blue light at Bleaklow

Bleaklow lies to the south of Holmfirth, a beautiful expanse of heather that looks towards Kinder Scout. I have a great regard for Bleaklow for it has always been cast as the underdog, over-shadowed by Kinder. Yet no one could conceal the exquisite elegance of this flat-topped fell on this September morning. My affection for Bleaklow has developed over many years, a product of its subtle character, its swathes of purple heather and sienna bracken. I often look in wonder at the hues of purple that melt in the distance into hazy, misty blues. As I placed my signature upon this work, I knew I had captured forever that dazzling, awe-inspiring September morning.

6

Rain on Flushhouse Moor

This painting brings back happy memories of the Ford Inn, Holmfirth, when Ken and Derek ran it. Those were the days when a public house was a public house; where anyone was at once made to feel welcome. On this particular day I had walked up the A635 to the Ford from Holmfirth. I turned left at the junction and on to the road to Flushhouse Moor. As I was about to begin sketching, the heavens opened so I retreated to the Ford. It was a poor excuse, really, as painting in the rain was something I was accustomed to. But my will-power had been weakened by the aroma of frying gammon on my way past the pub. Ken and Derek welcomed me with not one, but two bowls of homemade soup and a bacon sandwich followed by a good pint of ale. I thought I might be in the inn all day, as the weather had by now turned quite blustery.

Fortified by a second pint, however, I decided, "jigger the weather", and walked confidently out of the warm pub and into the bleak elements. For every step forward the wind sent me two steps back, but my battle was worth it: the scene on Flushhouse Moor, with its heavy, daunting and electrifying skies, overwhelmed me this time. I crouched for protection by the side of a drystone wall and took out my board and watercolours. I had to smile at this point as the words of my friend and old boss, Ron Darwent, came to mind. On days when the weather was bad and we were out signwriting a shop front, he would say: "As long as it is not raining on the job, but on us, we can work all right!"

Being an artist I paint vertically. Fortunately the rain, when you are high on the moors, hits you horizontally. I was getting drenched, yet my paper, miraculously, remained dry, for the rain was hitting only the back of my board. That said, it was still difficult to paint in these conditions. The wind was not just blowing, but billowing around me and I had to hold my board firmly with one hand while trying to paint with the other. It was all worth it, though, for a window in the sky had appeared and a shaft of light was shimmering through. I decided this was the moment I wanted to freeze in time. I would like to think that when you look at this painting it will induce a feeling of hope and the thought that every cloud *does* have a silver lining.

Some may consider this work and wonder why I should be inspired by such a miserable day. It is the rare and precious moments – like the window in the sky – that make it worthwhile, transforming a gloomy day into a brilliant one. I never view life pessimistically, I always look for hope; the day I stop doing so will be the day I draw my last breath on this beautiful planet. I try to put everything into perspective. Some people look at wine and see the bottle half empty; I see it as half full.

You may be able to guess why I dedicated this painting to my old journalist friend, John Thorpe, for it was he who dubbed me 'the patron saint of telegraph poles'. I would like to believe that the glimmer of hope I felt when viewing the vista shines through to you too.

7

Spotlight on the moor

I was allured to this beguiling and atmospheric scene of the dark, menacing, threatening and broody sky silhouetted against the shadowy mystique of the moorland uplands, by the heavenly windows of the earth's skylight. This shone shafts of light onto the overcast heath, illuminating it like a stage set, with the two main sheep the leading actors in this fine performance. I loved the electric atmosphere that surrounded me as I stood transfixed to the scene. The luminous and luscious cluster of yellow moorland lured me across the landscape towards the sheep who, as the clouds swept hurriedly across the skyline, appeared like boulders set on the horizon. I knew that these patches were not fresh and innocent grass as they appeared and in fact were moorland sponges enticing you and then swallowing you up, as your boots became sodden and your socks squelchy.

I used a little artistic licence in this painting, lifting onto the skyline the old Roman-style fortress and landmark of Huddersfield, Castle Hill. In reality this folly lay just below my horizon. I felt that if I was to look upon this view as a performance, the folly deserved a part. For like an old and established actor giving a guest performance in a play, the folly had once played a very important role in the accomplishment of the Industrial Revolution, acting as a watchtower and meeting place for the Luddites who established not only the county but its people in a very prominent spotlight which was to change the role of, and respect for, the working class for ever.

Suddenly I was reminded of the day in 1968 when the great L S Lowry walked unannounced into my gallery and purchased a painting entitled *Where Counties Meet*. Needless to say, it was a momentous landmark, for he became my mentor, offering good – often sharply realistic – advice and views on the world of art. I still hold his words in utmost respect. As I reappraised this painting, it was fascinating to think that this old man, who specialised in depicting stylised, industrial townscapes, was buying a painting of an empty moorland scene, devoid of people, from a young artist of 28. His death in February, 1976, was a great loss to the art world and to me. I had lost a guiding light in my struggle as an artist. It is for this reason that I chose to dedicate this painting to the memory of the incomparable L S Lowry.

8

No Thru Road – Wessenden Moor

I was drawn to choose this painting because, with its low, white clouds set against a cold February morning full of snow, shining and reflecting like a beautiful crystal into the sky, it represents and typifies a beautiful, cold winter's day; the kind that makes one realise that life is well and truly worth living. Standing on the moors, for me there is no joy that equals the gift of seeing: to witness the wind driving from the east, bending the tufts of grass, making them dance like Indian headdresses on the landscape; the moorland wall traversing across to a broken gate where one post stands, the solitary telegraph pole, the pearl blue sky hanging Mother Nature's virginal white necklace of clouds low. Before me was a sight and a real gift from Mother Nature herself that I could not ignore and had to capture. I was engulfed in the frozen sea, the telegraph pole appeared like the mast of a sinking ship that had been consumed by the power of the swell, and was leading and beckoning me to have a look at nature's treat. It was indeed a sight for my eyes.

I wanted to capture the crispness and cold of the day, but I also desired to portray the sheer bitterness, too. I wanted to be able to relive the feeling of the forbiddingness of the day, where the wind was chilling my bones through and draining my last breath from my body whenever I inhaled the fresh intoxicating air of the morning. It was as if she was allowing me the privilege of viewing and admiring her beauty, but she was not giving me this privilege without pain; like the bird swooping across the winter wonderland who was also being allowed the honour of taking in Mother Nature's all-consuming beauty, but at the same time fighting for survival. This painting is the epitome of the fine line that lies between pleasure and pain, and allows me to appreciate the true joy of seeing.

9

Drifting snow above Wessenden

On putting my signature to *No Thru Road*, the final brush stroke of any of my works, I was still left, despite the freezing chill of the day, aching to absorb more of the beauty of the day. I could not get enough of the exhilarating mood of the moor. I was standing here in true solitude; even the birds, who earlier had been swooping around me in search of food, had long since gone and left me at peace and at one with my moorland. I felt that morning as though Heaven was on Earth; my eyes drifted over this vista, hooked to the spot where the sky and land met. My rainbow's end, my paradise, my spiritual escapism lay in the far distance on the opposite side of the wall to where I had moments ago painted. The sheer brilliance of the moving light was transfixing me to a spot on the stark, dark stone wall with its heavy colours and tones contrasting heavily against the sea of white, with its crystal shades of blue reflecting upon it from the clear blue, calm sky above. The spiky, needle sharp tufts of grass, having survived the heavy fall of snow the previous night yet again attracted me. They appeared to be almost mocking the elements, laughing and dancing in the biting wind. But it was the route to my escapism that drove me to capture this sister painting to *No Thru Road*, for it is only when one views this spiritual place that one truly realises just how insignificant man really is. It is, indeed, a humbling yet uplifting experience to stand on the moor with a brush in your hand, capturing what you believe in your heart to be the essence and spirit of the moor, becoming so absorbed that you could hear a snowflake fall. That's a gift bestowed on me that I never can or will take for granted. I was absorbed from within, she touched my soul. And the only way I could repay her was to capture her pure divine beauty on my watercolour paper, and thus evolved *Drifting snow*. Like two siblings, I know you will be able to appreciate why I had to place not one, but both paintings in my book — they were conceived together and together they should remain.

Blackshaw Edge – Hebden Moor

"Strange, but true" is the line that enters my mind when I look at this painting, for it rekindles an unforgettable memory. It all began one day in 1978 when I was on Blackshaw Edge trying to record the scene: a windswept moor with farm buildings silhouetted on the horizon by a dark and forbidding sky. When I am out, it is rare that I see anyone else, except for the occasional farmer coming to check what I am doing on his land, or a passing hiker. On this particular day, however, I was met by an old gypsy woman wearing a shawl and tightly-plaited hair. Because I had been so engrossed, I had been unaware of her approach so I was somewhat startled when a voice said "Hello". She had brought over some goose eggs and it was while she was looking at my half-finished work that she announced that she could read a lot from it. She said that she could tell I had Spanish origins; I automatically took a keen interest, for her words were indeed true. I had a grandmother who had been a flamenco dancer. She said that it was the dark sombre colours which gave this away, likening them to those used by Velasquez and El Greco. She went on to predict that I would have a television programme based on my life, and a book, too. I took this with a pinch of salt and carried on painting, though I was drawn to her soft dialect as she continued to tell me about her life. She had lived for many years on a nearby farm. Becoming absorbed in my painting and enjoying the music of the moor echoing around me, I was unaware of her leaving. The music this day was provided by wind blowing through the telegraph wires. It would not be long before rain, as I could see that a cloud had burst to my left in the distance. Hurriedly I put on my waterproofs as I was not going to be deterred by rain from finishing this wonderful scene. I had fallen in love with the sight of the building with its ramshackle, undulating roof and higgledy-piggledy windows.

I was pleased with my final painting and I decided to go in search of the gypsy, not only to thank her for the eggs but to show her my work. I went across to the farm, but there was no trace. I thought no more of it, or the conversation we had, until a year later when an astonishing thing happened – her prophecy came true. Yorkshire Television producer Barry Cockcroft made a programme for his network series, *Once in a Lifetime*, about myself, my roots, and my attempt to trace them to Spain. The programme was called *My Own Flesh and Blood*. Six months later, publishers Secker and Warburg asked me to write my autobiography, *My Brush With Fortune*. I decided to go in search of the woman, and tell her my good news. I went to the exact spot and farm, but again I could not find her, so I decided to ask at a neighbouring farm. The farmer told me that he could recall no gypsy woman ever living up there, and he had lived there all his life. If it had not been for my goose eggs I might have thought I had imagined the whole story. To this day – and I have revisited numerous times since – I have never met this woman again.

II

Horsehouse – Dales

'Some days are diamonds and some days are stone'. These words spring to mind when I revisit a work conceived early in my career as a newly-married professional artist. For indeed, as I tried to capture the sparkling crystals of the Dales hamlet after a summer cloudburst, it was a truly diamond day. And no matter that rain had fallen: I find more enthusiasm striving to portray the ambience of a wet day than the often flat sky of a fine one. I have spent many an hour in the villages and towns of the Dales. They hold a very soft spot in my heart. I loved the area so much that I even bought a static caravan in Hawes for my young family to visit. It stood on Mrs Hessledeen's farm and a lovelier woman you could not choose to meet. She was the epitome of a Daleswoman: homely and plump with a heart of gold and an inner beauty that shone through. We would visit the Dales often. Sometimes Anne and the girls would play in the fields and go for long walks, leaving me to capture the spirit and character of these lovely surroundings. Although some critics have called me "a commercial artist" – a term that personally offends me, for I have only ever painted to please myself, and capture many a painting that one could admire but may have no desire to purchase and hang on one's wall, as it could seem either too cold or lonely – I have never felt the impulse to capture the Dales as so many artists have done, as chocolate box art. It's not that I object to such painters, it is just that I have never perceived the Dales in this way. I have seen a beauty beyond flowers climbing around stone porches and the heat of the sun cracking the pavements as a cat sits in a window box. But these sorts of days do not inspire me. Rather, I get excited when, like on this painting, the rain makes the road shine like the underside of a milk top, reflecting and crystallising the shape of the cottages. Colours cannot be brighter or stronger than when it has just stopped raining. I was equally fascinated by the glow in the sky as the clouds wrung out their last reluctant drops. To smell the freshness straight after rain is a wonder that never ceases to amaze me. I have included this study not only because it is an early favourite, recalling memories of youth, but as a reminder of some glorious times spent with my wife and daughters clothed in sou'westers and wellingtons, exploring the hidden gems of the Dales.

12

Bill's O' Jacks

Having lived for many years in Holmfirth – and having heard many of the stories and legends of the valley – I have rarely been as intrigued by a location as this site. Bill's O' Jacks, despite its isolation, was a famous pub that overlooked Wessenden and Saddleworth Moor in the heart of the Pennines. Sadly, it was pulled down many years ago. Mr and Mrs Bottomley, a lovely old local couple, would spend many an hour in my local tavern, The Elephant and Castle, relating the history and intrigue of this fascinating place – the scene of at least one murder. Local legend insists that it was one of the locations where Myra Hindley and Ian Brady planned their evil deeds on this moor. One day the Bottomleys brought to my gallery a couple of photographs that they had taken, years before, of this pub. Curiosity overtook me as I studied these sepia works. I needed to go and see for myself the ruin of the inn to discover whether its spirit would enfold me as I stood amid its foundations. I was not disappointed. I had intended to capture the location, as it is now – a ruin on the moor – but as I reached the position, and reconstructed in my mind's eye the building from the photograph, I felt that I would be doing an injustice. The site was pleading with me to capture it as it had stood for generations, in its own strange glory, away from the crowds: a refuge for refreshment, comfort – and intrigue. I rarely paint from photographs, believing them to taint the true, all-seeing eye, but this was an exception and I attempted to recreate this unspoiled environment, anxious to grasp its dark ambience. Even though I have tried to capture the moor in sombre mood with the hills fading into a dark sky, the rain sweeping across the barren landscape and the Greenfield reservoir in the distance, this location, set inhospitably between Holmfirth and Saddleworth, was once a refuge where a fire would have greeted travellers on a cold and dismal night. It was for this reason that I chose to put in a line of washing, blowing in the blustery wind to represent the truth that life goes on. Although this stretch of moorland can feel inhospitable, even on a summer day, I wanted to underline its natural beauty. To my good fortune, the light that day had a powerful, refractive quality, offering a whole range of possibilities to my palette. One cannot, despite its dark secrets, help but admire this desolate territory. The moors were not made evil; it is man that has made them so.

13

Birds over West Nab

This farm, lying majestically on West Nab overlooking the Colne Valley, looks and has always looked when I have passed it as though it is the cat that has got the cream. Here it stands, set proud against the skyline, high and exposed yet commanding a magnificent view. It holds through its windows a view and panorama to die for, looking in the distance towards Huddersfield and Wakefield. Although the house is no longer lived in it stands dignified, facing the elements in its monumental glory, holding within its walls the laughter of children from bygone years. One can almost imagine its pride at housing the generations, keeping them warm and safe, protecting them from the elements. I have admired this house for so many years that I felt this day compelled to finally capture her, as the sheep grazed so peacefully in the shadow of her presence. And yet it wasn't the house that totally inspired me to put brush to paper, nor was it the wonderful light that shone so strongly around the sheep pens, illuminating and guiding the eye, inviting the eye to view the silhouetted gable end, nor was it the sheep, nestled contentedly into the moorland grass. It was in fact the halo of light that had formed under the heaviness of the sienna sky, where hawks were flying, that was the true essence and the inspiration for the painting. They were flying and swooping in the area of my desires, my spiritual escape point – a point where mind and soul is led and where one can disappear into one's own thoughts and dreams, an area that I desire to be drawn to, and engulfed by. They were displaying an enviable freedom, and I was sharing with them, as an artist, the true solitude of the day, hoping and wishing that my thoughts can and will intermingle forever.

14

Low Row, Swaledale

Swaledale is my favourite Yorkshire Dale, for it lacks the candy floss that is cynically exploited in some of the others. Here you see the fells in their unadorned beauty. I discovered Swaledale over 35 years ago with my young wife, Anne, when we camped at Gunnerside. We would trek up from Barnsley for weekends, moving on to Muker. A favourite haunt was The Farmers Arms at Muker, a small inn set back from the road with its toilets across the road. It always amused us that you could get killed crossing the road in an inebriated state, going to relieve yourself! Donald France, the landlord, was a character and often spoke about his army life in India. We became quite friendly and would help out, serving in a very busy pub during Muker Show. On one of our visits, he invited us to take his horse, Starlight, on to the fells for exercise. My wife rode her up the fell, me holding the lead rein, in full view of the village and the pub. After a while Anne and I got into a heated dispute as to whose turn it was to ride. Feeling like John Wayne – we lads from Barnsley are a little bit macho – I would show Anne how to really ride a horse and how to sit in the saddle. My great chance came to ride back down the fell. The moment I put my foot in the stirrup and tried to hoist myself into the saddle, young Starlight took it in her mind to show me a thing or two by bolting down the fell side. At this point I had one foot in the stirrup and was running with the other foot on the ground, shouting and swearing at her to stop. I managed to free my foot from the stirrup, but my hand was fastened in the rein. Starlight was now heading at great speed for home while I was trying to wedge the heels of my shoes into the stones and boulders to slow us down. The horse was having none of this. Vaguely aware of a Wallace Arnold coachload of tourists, I ended up at the front door of The Farmers Arms with no heels on my scuffed and muddied boots. Needless to say, I was greeted by Donald, laughing with all the customers. Starlight still had another gem to deliver. An open-topped beer barrel full of water was kept at the door just for the horse; however, one nudge from her flanks and I was wedged in the barrel, soaking wet! I looked round to see Anne running down the fell side laughing hysterically. While painting "Low Row" I could not forget that day in Muker, as the far fell in this painting reminded me of Starlight – happy days!

15

Hannah Hauxwell's farm – Low Birk Hatt

I include this painting in honour of a special person I had the privilege to meet, a woman who came to public knowledge through the award-winning documentary *Too Long A Winter*. On meeting her and talking with her, she reflected through her soul everything that I love about Yorkshire and her moors. Here was a woman who had weathered everything the elements had thrown at her; a woman I knew was at one with my spirit of the county, Hannah Hauxwell. It was a summer day that my friend, the cameraman Mostafa Hamuri, took me to Low Birk Hatt Farm, high on the isolated moors above Teesdale. To my dying day, I will never forget my inspiring encounter with 'the lady of the moor'. As the door opened I was met by a white-haired, rosy-cheeked woman – a scarf tied tight around her head, a sacking apron, old, but clean, around her waist, wellingtons on her feet – carrying a pail of water. Although we had called unannounced, we were met on this cool day by a wonderful warm smile that beckoned us in. The harshness of Hannah's life had been etched in her features. Many people would have struggled to imagine, let alone survive, the prospect of life without electricity, gas or running water. Her seasoned, wrinkled face – burnt by the winds, blistered by the sun, her bleached hair held in a neat bun – were a living epitaph to the elements. Yet for all that her life had been harsh, her eyes still held the brightness and innocence of youth. They held you, drawing you into them, and I immediately felt as if I had known this woman all my life. She had the quiet aura of one in whose presence I could relax; talk about any subject I desired, ask any question I liked.

Although I had known her for barely an hour, I asked Hannah a question that one might shrink from asking a life-long friend. And yet I knew that here was a woman who would not be offended, but respect my enquiry. I asked Hannah – living so close to nature and the controlling force, yet miles away from any place of worship – whether she was a religious person. She poignantly answered: "One doesn't need to look through a stained glass window to be religious, I worship in the great cathedral of the open air." This sentence etched itself deeply on my soul – I knew exactly what she meant, for I, too, shared that philosophy. I realised then that she too was captured and captivated by the power of the natural landscape. Here stood a woman before me, that I knew could comprehend my thoughts on my life and the county that inspired them. Whenever I look at my painting of Hannah's farm, her home, her life, I know that here once lived and breathed a woman who embodies everything that I strive to capture through my watercolours – the spirit of the moor.

16

Soft light over Yorkshire

I have always had a sweet affection for Calderdale. It was Calderdale, in fact, which gave me the honour of my first exhibition at what was then the Liberal Party headquarters, Brighouse, in January 1965. I was just 29. I hold the area close to my heart, in particular the moor above Halifax over which I have spent many an hour trekking. Hiking one day over Widdings Moor, I came across this vista which made the hairs on the back of my hand stand rigid and my spine tingle. I knew immediately that I had to capture this moment – the moor in its glory. This view depicts, to my mind, everything of Yorkshire: farms clinging to moorland uplands, verdant valleys, stone walls traversing the moor making a lovely patchwork of the landscape, dead trees tracing lace patterns against the sky and electricity poles, emblems of the modern age. The Yorkshire moors are a challenge to any artist. To my mind their character is harder to register than the mountain areas of Scotland and Wales. Mountains are pyramids and if you think like this they become easy to paint, especially in a group, for they offer ready-made perspective and instant depth. But the Yorkshire moorlands, in particular Widdop, are high but set at slight angles. The challenge is to make them appear to lie down, a task which sets my adrenalin flowing. The beauty of the moors, too, is that because of their layout they create large and powerful skies, which assist me in capturing the dramatic and often windswept beauty of Yorkshire.

17

Upper Knowles Farm

As I put brush to paper to capture Upper Knowles Farm, the words of Tennyson's poem, *The Deserted House,* came floating into my mind,

Come away: for life and thought
Here no longer dwell.
But in a city glorious –
– A great and distant city –
have bought
A mansion incorruptible.
Would they could have stayed with us.

Every time I view this work, I hear the echo of these words. Although the farm appears derelict, I felt as though its walls were beckoning me closer to tell the tales of those who had lived within its walls. I could almost hear the laughter of playing children, the clatter of milk churns, the sounds of the sheep being gathered in. Despite the place being desolate, a gritty spirit enlivened this farm and its fields; a spirit that epitomised the strength of character of those who toiled down the generations to make a living and a life from the land. They are – and will always be – the backbone of true Yorkshire, for they endured all that life tossed at them. I hope that their gritty spirit echoes in this hanging 'epitaph' to the lives of those it once housed.

To reach Upper Knowles Farm, take the A635 out of Holmfirth onto Wessenden Head, and where the road doubles back on itself, you can see the farm on your left hand side over a long green track. I believe the site is still used by Scouts as a weekend and adventure cottage. It could not be more brilliantly situated, as it lies within easy access of Holme Moss, the Pennine Way and many more challenging walks. Oh to be a young boy once more...

18

Cold and damp on Bradshaw Moor

I have always had a romantic fascination for the Yorkshire uplands, where the moors penetrate the skies. There is a glory to them even in the most apparently unpromising of conditions when the wind hectors and the drizzle chastens. It was this mood of the moor that captivated me back in 1984, one of her autumnal days. I desperately tried to capture all that Bradshaw was trying to convey on this cold, damp September morning. This was possibly my last chance to see it under the lushness that a wet summer had unexpectedly bestowed. It had given me a few more weeks to wait in eager anticipation for the autumnal colours to show their glory. The atmosphere that day was of solitary splendour. It was as though everyone had gone to town and no one had returned. To many this would be disturbing but I was in my element. This is how I like to be when I am painting, all alone, with no one to disturb me. This may appear selfish but it is the only way I can record the ambience of the moor for others. I often say that some days are diamonds and others are coal; this was truly a diamond day, and beyond doubt deserved to be in this special collection of what amount to my visual love letters.

19

Open moorland

I felt compelled to add this work, conceived in the late 70s, as a symbol of the raw and naïve style of painting that I felt in my soul. Many of my paintings during this period were done from a worm's eye view. As I lay on the ground with my easel and paints, I imagined myself as a grouse nestling within the bracken and heather, capturing in watercolour, with my dry brush, the grass as it shot above my head into the expanse of the open sky. I look upon these works and reflect fondly upon their simplicity, which is beautiful. I recollect the damp grass of the August morning on a bright jewel of a day. One cloud of the purest white floated by, like a Man O' War moving gracefully across the sky in full sail, contrasting magnificently against the azure space. This painting embodies all the youth, energy, pride and passion of my twenties; all the fervour and strength that could be found within the soul of a Yorkshireman. It was for this reason that when Dodworth Brass Band asked if they could use one of my paintings on the cover of their new album, I had no hesitation in choosing this. The band will always hold a special place in my heart. I was brought up in Barnsley, and the stirring sounds of brass symbolised the strength, warmth and power of a community held together by coal. As a young boy I would often listen to the evocative melodies flowing from the band room, wondering how men who spent their days digging for Barnsley's gold could produce such beguiling music that could seduce the most philistine of ears. I learned at an early age that music and art were wonderful forms of escapism, and, as a young boy toiling over my watercolours, I was doing exactly what any members of the band were doing, escaping through their music from their mundane and often harsh life into a world exciting and undiscovered… their inner soul. I was later honoured to become the band's vice president, a position I held with pride until the catastrophic closure of the mines put paid to many such ensembles. On viewing this work, I reflect on what I shared with all those young miners: energy, strength and surety; the defining attributes of a young Yorkshireman. As George Bernard Shaw said, "It is unfortunate that youth is wasted on the young." But I also contemplate this painting with sadness for what man's greed and exploitation has done to this fiercely proud community. The drive and raw determination that could be found not just in my heart and soul but within the miners of Barnsley had sadly been destroyed, bludgeoning their spirit in such a way that it can never return. Never again will a cornet be heard from the band room. The courage, fervour and soul of the men were sacrificed by a government without feeling. How lucky I am to be an artist, for art knows no political barriers and no man will ever be able to drive the passion for my vocation from my bones.

20

Wild moor

This is the sister to the painting *Open moorland* – a pair that holds a special place in my heart; it was featured on the second album cover of Dodworth Brass Band. I dedicate them both, in this book, to the men and women not only of Barnsley, but all those other towns that lost their spirit and drive with the closure of the mines. Whenever I glance at these works, I can almost smell the freedom of spirit that I felt as a young artist. I think of the grouse in August which, in mid-flight, were momentarily free from the hunters' aim and would live to see another day. The rain was falling on this August day, yet the sun was shining. If you inspect the work closely, you can detect in the foreground the drops that fell, helping me with the formation of my clumps of grass and bracken. Although *Wild moor* and *Open moorland* to some eyes can appear raw and naïve, I look upon them with great admiration in my strive for perfection.

21

Wash day blues – some things will never change

I was drawn to this scene in Deepdale, Upper Wharfedale, on a fine clear day. The air was fresh, cool and invigorating and new-born lambs were bleating all around. Spring had at last arrived. When I came across this homestead, with the washing billowing in the wind, I knew life could not get much better. There was nothing for it but to put brush to paper and capture the view. Whenever I look at this painting, I can smell the freshness of that day. It also raises a smile, as I will explain... Some hours later, not far from the scene of this painting, a police car pulled me over and the officer asked if I had been in Wharfedale. I told him I had. What, he asked, had I been doing? I quickly explained that I'd been painting. He looked a shade embarrassed as it dawned who I was! It transpired that my registration number had been taken by a neighbour of the house I had been painting, and I had been reported as acting suspiciously. We both laughed about the episode and I went on my way thinking no more – until that night, when the telephone rang. It was the owner of the house apologising profusely for the mistake. I told her not to worry: the enjoyment of depicting her home far outweighed the temporary embarrassment at being thought a felon! The pure, unashamed naïvety of this scene makes me hope that future generations will be able to have and appreciate similar ones. Let us pray that in this new century some things will never change.

Emmerdale – 1998

This painting of *Emmerdale*, the purpose-built location for Yorkshire Television's network series, was commissioned by Yorkshire Television for its boardroom. Although I rarely undertake commissions, I felt proud that the company had chosen me and I accepted the invitation in tribute to the 30 years' association I have enjoyed with it. For like my wife, who had faith in me from the beginning, Yorkshire Television has been a loyal supporter. The first programme I featured in was the award-winning documentary *It's No Joke Living in Barnsley* which also included Dickie Bird, Charlie Williams, Arthur Scargill, Dorothy Hyman and Brian Glover. We were all starting out and I am proud to be able to say that we all made the grade, establishing ourselves over some 20 years in our chosen fields. A few years later Sid Waddell, a director renowned for his darts commentaries, asked me to take part in a *Calendar* documentary about the life of William Scorsby, the painter and whaler from Whitby. This remarkable figure invented the crow's nest and designed the lifeboat and its means of suspension over the side of the ship. It was my job to emulate the style of his work – a big challenge. A young broadcaster by the name of Richard Whiteley, still years away from *Countdown* success, was to provide the voice-over. As the years went by, director Barry Cockcroft, who rose to fame through some fine documentaries, chose to devote a programme to tracking my Spanish roots entitled *My Own Flesh and Blood*. The research and the

subsequent book, *My Brush with Fortune*, gave me an insight into many unanswered parts of my life. Indeed, the whole experience was to prove a personal milestone, for at last I knew who I was, where I had come from, and where I was going. I felt a sense of belonging and for that I have Yorkshire Television and Barry Cockcroft to thank. It also represented a significant career break in terms of television, as it led to my own show, *A Brush With Ashley* – now in its eighth series. I have striven all my life to make my work accessible; Yorkshire Television has given me the platform to pursue that ambition. My belief is that art should be for everyone, not just the elite, and I will always be indebted to that company for allowing me to fulfil this desire. Television, though, is like the candles on a cake in my career. I am completely aware of the industry's capacity to suck you in, chew you up and then spit you out. I count myself lucky to be part of this exciting medium, safe in the knowledge that I can keep my feet firmly on the ground – for I remain foremost an artist. There is a huge difference between a television artist and an artist who appears on television. Art is my life and will remain so until the day I die.

23

Staithes

There are some lovely fishing villages on the east coast of Yorkshire. Nestling in the shoulders of its huge cliffs, lies one: Staithes. The area is steeped in maritime history: Captain James Cook worked as a boy just up the road before going to sea. I was attracted to Staithes with its clusters of white fishermen's cottages, like penguins on an Icelandic coast, looking out to sea. This painting grew out of my Yorkshire Television series *A Brush With Ashley* which was great fun to work on. As I painted this scene, I could almost sense the apprehension of fishermen putting out into inhospitable seas. For all their differences, there's a chilling parallel between the moors and the seas. You can go out on either in the spirit of recreation or adventure and within moments the weather can change so dramatically as to put your life at risk. The fishermen who go out to bring in their catch know full well that they could be sacrificing their lives. As I worked on this painting on a warm summer day, with seagulls silhouetted against still skies, I felt that this lovely, historic fishing village held many secrets.

I tried to paint the rocky foreground with its piles of modern cut concrete along the shoreline, breakers to an unforgiving North Sea. The traditional fishermen's cottages, with their caps of red pantile roofs standing firm against the wind and elements, formed the perfect contrast. Yes, it is a truly lovely, unspoilt village; I relished my day at Staithes.

24

Dusk creeps in over the moor – Saddleworth Moor

To see the spirit of Yorkshire and its moors
Through your eyes is one thing;
Many people look but only a few see,
And feel its very soul.
For, out of the monochrome mist,
You will feel the movement of the moor.
It is the moors to me that make life,
Make life interesting and important.
I know of no substitute, to paint
With heart and, most of all, soul,
The beauty and force it possesses.

LINES FROM MY SKETCHBOOK

25

Nature's power – Greenfield Moor in winter

It is only with the heart that one can see rightly; what is essential is invisible to the eye.

ANTOINE DE SAINT EXUPÉRY *THE LITTLE PRINCE*

26

The eye, the heart and the moor – West Nab

The true measure of the artist is that he is constantly measuring himself against eternity.

STEPHEN SPENDER

27

Moorland windows in the sky

I know we are herd people, we feel safe in a crowd, but I am one who feels at one with the moor, alone. Yet, I never feel alone when I paint with the music of the wind and the tears of rain that touch my face with joy.

ASHLEY JACKSON 1999

28

Heather on the jewelled moor – West Nab and Deer Hill

Years go by as fast as cat's eyes on a motorway. The art of living is to make use of what you've got, and use it to the full. Most people don't know what they are living for. But once you have found out, you have the jewel of life.

ASHLEY JACKSON 1999

29

Angry sky

While wandering above Farndale in North Yorkshire, I came across this lonely rowan tree, fighting against the odds to survive. Indeed, the theme of the scene was survival: the wild, unforgiving sky set against wet, boggy moorland, the stark lonely tree still breathing life as sheep grazed, oblivious to another approaching storm, made me feel humble. To depict flat moorland, high above sea level and to capture light reflecting and refracting on the landscape is a constant challenge. If it is not executed properly it can give the impression of marshland – the Norfolk fens, for instance – rather than the high reaches of the Yorkshire Moors. This painting holds a special place for another reason. It was the first that my eldest daughter, Heather, saw after returning from travelling the world for a year. I had asked her six months before whether she would consider becoming my manager. She maintains that it was this painting that convinced her to work with me, saying that any man who could bare his soul in such a powerful and evocative way and expose it for all to see and criticise was in need of a manager to protect and care for him. Neither of us has looked back and we owe much to this piece of work.

30

Tranquillity in Farndale

I have chosen this painting for two reasons. Firstly for my admiration and love of Farndale and secondly as a tribute to my friend, boss and mentor – and best man! – Ron Darwent. I owe him a great debt, for it was he who in my youth took me onto the moors and shared with me the pure, unadulterated joy of her spirit. I often still go out walking with Ron, sketching but never painting, for I can never paint in the presence of anyone, selfishly wanting to covet the scene for myself. I have often likened painting to writing a love letter – and, just as one cannot compose a love letter in public, the same applies to painting. Your whole mind, body and soul must be engrossed. It was on one of our walking expeditions that I sketched this scene of an old gnarled elm by a quiet lane, overlooking Farndale, its wooded glades reflecting their colour into the afternoon sky. I worked in pain, for we had just come down from the fells and, believing that I was still as agile as a young buck, I jumped from a stile on to the footpath, losing my balance and twisting my ankle. The experience underlined the harsh reality that I was 50, and I knew instinctively that I had badly damaged my foot. But Ron, being Ron, an experienced mountaineer and climber, convinced me that I had "nowt but sprained it", so we continued for a further six miles to this vista. This typical English scene with its hedges and pastures was wonderfully attractive; the light playing on it emphasised the contrast of foreground, horizon and middle distance. The foreground was strong in colour and tone, reminding me of an old master's oil painting, yet the middle and far distance were soft and misty, akin to an oriental watercolour. Unlacing my boot when I got home that evening I realised that my instinct had been correct; I had broken my ankle. The next day, with a pot encasing my foot, I set about uncorking memories of the previous day. As I recreated the scene it dawned that, subconsciously, I had translated the pain into my sketches; somehow it had enhanced the scene. I still believe to this day that the wonderful glow of the summer light was enhanced by the experience. As I finished the painting amid the comfort of my studio, I decided that *Tranquillity in Farndale* was the perfect title for a painting that embodied an experience that had been anything but!

31

Wessenden Valley

My approach to painting when I am in the open air is to let the landscape come to me – and then go with it. If it does not do that, I walk on, for I want to create a painting not a picture. When out one day on Wessenden Moor, I found that the evocative fragrances of wild flowers, heather and burnt bracken were enhancing my senses. My sight, my smell, my hearing all seemed crystal clear as I stood looking down into the valley. The landscape was beckoning and I did not want the moment to pass. I wanted to spread my arms and swoop like a great condor in flight, absorbing the sheer beauty of it all, seizing it and freezing it forever. The moors below gave the illusion of huge mammals basking shoulder to shoulder in the sun and, as I put paint to paper, I tried to portray this image. The scene was one of contentment and peacefulness, for in the words of Thomas Hardy I felt I was "far from the madding crowd". Who could believe that just around the corner lay the industrial panorama of Marsden and Meltham? That is one of the many virtues of Yorkshire: it takes just a few miles to find a high plateau, leave your world and troubles behind and look beyond the rainbow into your dreams.

Love who has us in his net
Can we dream and not forget?
For life is dreams.

When we who stand on the moor
See dreams of bygone life, for sure
We see ourselves as ourselves,
And not as people see us.

Love who has us in his net
Has given us dreams
We can't forget.

So be human!
Feel the land – for the land
Will feel us all one day,
For life is dreams which we
Will not regret.

ASHLEY JACKSON 1968

32

Overcast skies

I have included this in the collection for a number of reasons. Firstly, it represents the essence of autumn, a wonderful season when one can savour rich, subtle siennas playing against winter greys, producing a cloak of vivid colour. Secondly, I liked the way the shades of light gave away the secrets of the moor, lightly touching the grazing sheep and brushing the stone buildings as they basked in the last rays of the summer sun. But chiefly I have chosen this painting because it typified a true Yorkshire home. It represents the many friendly and welcoming men and women who live in moorland farms, north, south, east and west of Yorkshire, all of whom have greeted me with a smile. Farmers and shepherds, men and women who work in the open air, possess a special character; life has carved for them qualities that glow from within. I recall painting a farm scene in the West Riding, not dissimilar to this (hence its inclusion), when a giant of a farmer approached. His manner and purposeful stride suggested he was going to tell me I was trespassing and to get off his land. Instead, he said: "My wife and I were watching you from the kitchen window and she sent me out to see what you are doing." He stood and watched as the image of his farm gradually took shape on the paper. He was a man of few words but I happened to mention that it was the sort of sunny day when one should have a pint of bitter in hand rather than a bucket of water containing your brushes. No sooner had I said it than he disappeared – only to return with two large ice-cold cans of beer. His wife had clearly been involved in this gift, for in his other hand were two large crystal tankards that sparkled in the summer sun. One cannot be made to feel more welcome in Yorkshire than sharing a pint of beer with a stranger out of his best cut-glass. I have included this painting as a tribute to the hospitality and warmth of those who have made me feel welcome while out on my painting expeditions.

33

The warmth of summer light at Hade Edge

I first discovered the enchanting Holme Valley some 40 years ago when I cycled from Barnsley with my stepfather's brother, Malcolm Haigh. As we were only a year apart in age, we looked upon each other as brothers rather than uncle and nephew. I was 15 and had already seen spectacular views in several countries. Due to the war, my mother and I had become evacuees from Malaya, where my father was in British intelligence. Our evacuation took us first to India, then Scotland, before we returned to Malaya, only to find that my father had been killed while a prisoner of war. My mother later remarried and we came back to Britain, first to Huddersfield, then later to Barnsley. Nothing, though, prepared me for the view that greeted us that day as the fair reward for cycling up to Woodhead and the strength-sapping incline to Holme Moss. Reaching its peak tired and exhausted, I planned to eat my sandwiches and drink my pop. But I struggled to do either as I was so overpowered by the overwhelming beauty of the Holme Valley. I can close my eyes now and recall the vivid scene, with the main valley and the smaller valleys channelling into it. The green fields with their drystone walls, the tall trees, the Alpine-like villages and hamlets that appeared to be clinging to the hills combined to give the appearance of a beautiful yet complex patchwork quilt. I longed to capture the scene, but I had not taken my sketchbook and pen. Little did I imagine that one day I would live here. For some 13 years after that day, I travelled regularly to the valley I had come to love. Aged 27, I was fortunate enough to be given a job as a further education tutor in art at Holmfirth Further Education Centre. This led me to meet a fabulous man, Duncan Haughey. Had it not been for him telling me about a property for sale, I might never have realised my dream of living in the Holme Valley. At 33, I became a "comer-in", and could now fully devote my time to discovering the joys of the landscape that surrounded me, the nooks and crannies of the moors where the summer wine did not flow! I originally titled this picture *Warmth of Summer Light, Hade Edge*, a view I caught in September, 1996, while out walking with my daughter, Heather. Normally in summer I find little inspiration in clear blue skies. But while climbing over the stile about 100 yards from the school, I was transfixed by the view. Much to the annoyance of my daughter I decided there and then to return to the car to collect my paints, and that was the end of our walk! My eye was drawn at once to the farm building built into the land side. It reminded me of the mountainous regions of Italy where farmhouses are sculpted into the hill. I particularly liked how the light of this September day was hitting the Yorkshire stone. While standing on the stile, I could – in spite of the haze, which tends to make you lose your perspective – see West Nab in the distance; if I climbed the banking opposite I would see Castle Hill. I decided I was going to use an artist's licence and import Castle Hill to the scene, a device Turner, often used when he was out painting.

34

The George at Hubberholme

I can recall the first time, in the early 1960s, that I came across
The George Inn at Hubberholme, a tavern I have visited many
times since. I had called in for some soup and a hot beef sandwich and I was amazed to find a man of the cloth standing
behind the bar, serving me with my pint of bitter. It transpired
that he was the Vicar of Hubberholme and that this pub was
owned by the Church of England, a thought that still fills me
with laughter. Were I a cartoonist, I would depict the pub as
Hell and the church as Heaven, with the regulars going over
the bridge to the church to pray that once they have confessed
their sins they will be allowed to return to their tavern without
falling into the river! Many artists have portrayed this popular
inn with its beautiful arched bridge over the Wharfe and the
appealing church on the other side. However, I wanted to
capture a different aspect; those familiar with the pub will
recognise the angle. I went across the Wharfe to the side of the
church and walked down the river bank until I was met with
this scene with tall trees and the culvert ferrying the intoxicating water from the fells to the Wharfe. The pub, with its
mullioned windows, the stone bridge, the trees dancing in the
spring breeze, and the narrow road winding towards the mist-
shrouded fell symbolised the changelessness and tranquillity of
the Dales. This is my tribute to a part of the county I have
grown to adore.

35

Racehorse Inn, Kettlewell

This painting, I am proud to say, hangs in the Ashley Jackson Gallery at Barnsley College, the site of my old art school. No greater accolade can be bestowed on an artist than to see a gallery established in his honour, and I was humbled when David Eade, chief executive of the college, came to my gallery to purchase works for students and the public to view and admire. When I was 23, I had seen a painting of this inn by my good friend, the late Angus Rands, whose work I had long admired. His works were often published in the *Dalesman* magazine alongside the likes of Fred Lawson, Percy Monkman, Tom Sykes, Joe Pighills and E J W Prior. I had visited this pub many times and regarded it as a gateway to the Dales. On this particular bright day, I knew precisely what I intended to paint, and from which angle, for Angus Rands had been here more than 30 years before. I slipped through an opening in the stone wall and came across my scene, with the River Wharfe meandering down the dale enjoying the lazy heat of the day. I delighted in the way the light was catching the tops of the foliage, casting deep cool shadows among the rich greens, yellows and blues that surround the pub, enhancing the dazzling white of its walls. This to me was England, and I was in my seventh heaven. It is with a great sense of pride that I include this painting; it represents one of my greatest achievements.

36

Scorched Earth – West Nab

Earth, Wind and Fire are elements I have always striven to portray. These next two paintings, conceived one summer day in 1991, represent my most powerful and evocative depictions of the elements to date. I was at my gallery in Holmfirth when I had word that West Nab was on fire. I knew I had to go immediately and witness this sight. Yearning throughout my life as an artist to capture every mood of the moor, I knew I had to get up onto her and witness for myself her struggle against the elements. With sketchbook in hand, I quickly drove the few miles out of Holmfirth. As I climbed the hill, a dark shadow hung over the horizon and I could smell the scorch of her burning bracken, but not yet see the fire. My feelings were strangely mixed: I was anxious to get to the location, yet nervous that the damage would be too much to bear. This, after all, was my moor that was dying. I wanted to be there – and yet I didn't. I could hear the urgent wail of fire engines coming up the valley to the moor. Yet when I reached the plateau of West Nab, the spectacle was not fearful at all. It was as though the moor had accepted with dignity that the fire was stripping her of her fine clothing, disrobing the purple heather and sienna bracken from her back, and yet she looked so majestic and graceful. As the fire lay bare her soul, she still epitomised the strong and wilful spirit I had grown so deeply and affectionately to love. I put pencil to paper, making two sketches which were to evolve into *Scorched Earth*, and *Earth, Wind and Fire*. Both were done on my large 40×26 inch watercolour paper, as I felt that I needed such a size to do justice to the passion and spirit I had witnessed. Technically, I found both paintings a huge challenge for I needed the wind-driven fire to weld into a sky which resembled a Red Indian's headdress – the feathers protruding into the clouds, the red glow on the horizon providing a wondrous headband. The deep gullies in the foreground offered the perfect composition, leading the eye to the fire. I perceived them as war trenches where men could wait for reinforcements as the battle progressed further down the line. The moorland wall on the horizon seemed to appear and disappear from view in the smoke and haze, something I tried to recreate on paper with the heavy pall casting a huge eerie shadow on to the moorland. It was like a cloak of death over her – yet I knew that for all this pain and suffering, she would rise again – and even more beautifully.

37

Earth, Wind and Fire

This sister painting to *Scorched Earth* is a jewel. The movement of light shining down on the moorland track that led to the fire intensified the lushness and illumination of the moor. It was as though the moor had resigned herself to the fact that in a few minutes she would succumb to fire, but before she was consumed, she would shine in her full glory for a final time. The green of the moor had never looked so beautiful, the distant fire lighting the skyline and the smoke shrouding the sky, highlighting the path further. I could hear the crackling of the peat and bracken and smell the earthiness of the tinder-dry peat burning; it would not be long before I was in the path of the flames. I hurriedly laid my final pencil strokes down onto the paper and headed for the security of my car, driving straight to my studio to decant the atmosphere and images etched on my mind. I wanted to leave nothing to the imagination. One cannot perfect such magnificence as I had the privilege of witnessing. I prayed that I would be able to do the moor the justice she deserved. As the smoke choked her and the flames licked, she still looked magnificent and my love for her grew even deeper.

38

Twilight of the Twentieth Century

I write this as the sands of time of the 20th century run out, and we all appear to be racing in hurried excitement towards the 21st century. But what, I often wonder, is it all about? What are we racing to? The mechanics of life are seemingly driving our generation faster and faster, leaving us with no time to stand and stare – what is all the rush? It was while in this melancholy mood that I decided to capture a painting which for me would represent "the last years" on God's earth, which many have taken for granted, feeling that we should not spend our time always looking to the future but live it now, appreciate every breath we take, the beauty, the countryside that we have been bequeathed. If I was to choose one moment in time that I could carry forth, this painting of Flight Hill above Holmfirth would be it. It was a pure joy to capture, and I hope that the jubilant mood I felt on this day has been portrayed to you. It depicts to my mind everything great about the 20th century; the beautiful unspoilt moorland with not a single building to be seen, the quiet empty road leading to nowhere, and the telegraph poles that represent the fantastic communication advances that man has made. The painting also epitomises and parallels my own life. I have had the rainy days, the stormy days and windy nights that have been so evocatively seen through my works of brooding skies and windswept moors. On the approach to my 60th birthday, I believe that I can finally say, yes, there are days on this earth that bask in glorious light with crystal clear and wispy skies that shine their heavenly light onto a carpet of moorland green. *Twilight of the Twentieth Century* was one of these jewelled days, and I dedicate this painting to the twilight years of the 20th century which have shadowed over me as an artist, and to those who unfortunately will not realise what we have in this world until it is too late.

Moorland Grit

Tennyson's words, "The purple in the distance dies", embody my feelings in 1985 when conceiving this study of Beamsley Beacon, near Bolton Abbey. The vista that day was beautiful; the heather had died back and the bracken was proudly displaying its fine rich sienna. It was as if someone had thrown a well-worn piece of Yorkshire cloth, in delicate tones of mauves, siennas and pastel greens, over the moors as far as the eye could see – a wondrous sight. I was intrigued by the mist clinging to the moor, as though reluctant to reveal its secrets, its beautiful becks and streams. Yet the foreground stood in stark contrast to the soft lyrical shades of the mist and heather, challenging me to capture this glory. The painting holds many fond memories; I wanted it to lead the viewer in through a tunnel of light, an echo. I wanted the scene to tell a story, inviting the eye to wander over the moor, then allowing the mind to escape into its own world, into the distance. As I worked, I was aware Turner had painted a similar scene close to this place some 200 years earlier. The sense of his presence was a further spur to my creativity. I have chosen this painting for two reasons. First, it is an area of immense beauty. Second, it summarises everything that I love about our country, not just the sheer beauty of it but the fact that, health aside, it allows you to do or be anything you want. As you will realise by now, for me, that has always been, to be an artist. How can this painting symbolise so much? Simple. It all started one teatime in 1989 with my wife and children. I told them that I would like to invite HRH The Prince of Wales to my forthcoming exhibition, *Ashley Jackson's Vision of Turner in Yorkshire*, that was to include this painting. They all looked at me as though to say, "And who do you think you are?" But I was not put off, I hurried my tea, and immediately wrote a letter, enclosing an invitation. To cut the story short, the results were beyond my wildest dreams, for the Prince actually ended up travelling to Huddersfield to open my exhibition. I relate this story not to boast or brag, but in a spirit of encouragement. Go out and be or do whatever you want in life; never for one moment doubt your own potential, believe in yourself. If you cannot believe in yourself how can you expect others to? Whenever I feel any doubt or lose my inner confidence, I take a look at this painting, and rejuvenate my spirit . . . living to fight another day.

40

Morning light – Marrick Priory

I first met Brighouse artist the late Stanley Chapman in the early 1960s at my first exhibition at Brighouse Liberal Club and we remained friends until his death. He was the only person that I would ever paint alongside in the open air. Never for a moment was there any sense of unease; we were two independent artists with a mutual respect and love for painting. I include this painting as a tribute to Stanley and his wife, Mary, who would often accompany us, sitting in the car with her knitting and book until we returned. She respected our love of painting and always left us to it, never once asking to join us. Stanley was with me when I painted this scene of Marrick Priory. I had spoken with him many times about my ambition to trace the footsteps of Turner, who came to this site 200 years ago on his great tour of the north. I wanted to revisit many of his locations and capture my interpretations for an exhibition that I had titled – long before my paintings were conceived – as *Ashley Jackson's Vision of Turner in Yorkshire*. Marrick Priory was one of those locations and Stanley accompanied me to this lovely abbey in Swaledale, a few miles from Richmond. In fact, I painted it from the other side of the river from that which Turner had done, though the scene had hardly changed from his day. You could almost imagine him riding around the corner on horseback to greet you. It was a peaceful summer day with white clouds rolling by, one of those idyllic days that you dream of and imagine your childhood to have been full of. But

as we began to paint one threatening black cloud appeared, its presence providing a wonderful light and tone to the scene. A true Turner-inspired location, the warmth of the sky with its oranges enthralled me and the browns reflecting on to the landscape evoked the tender spirit of this place. This affectionate light appeared to be guiding my eye on to the peaceful priory with its farm and cloistered environment. If I were asked to choose a painting from my collection that represented England in her finery, this would be it. The fells stand in the background, protecting the deep, flat dale from the elements and providing an aura of calm. You could almost close your eyes and imagine to the far side of the abbey a cricket field and hear the clunking of the ball as it hits the bat. Swaledale is said to be a favourite dale of the Prince of Wales and I have no doubt why. It truly is a hidden gem.

41

Cauldron Snout – hubble bubble toil and trouble

From the moment I set eyes on Turner's watercolour of Cauldron Snout in Teesdale, I longed to offer my own interpretation. With my friend Ron Darwent I set off one bleak winter morning to the Snout, from High Force, another site of Turner's paintings. Normally the journey takes about four hours but in this case, hampered by driving snow and high winds, we did not arrive until late afternoon. I have long believed that to be able to paint heaven, one must see hell, and the Snout was the nearest I will come to it – in this life, at least! I was awestruck and dumbfounded at the view. The noise and power of the water thundering in the gorge was deafening. I could almost hear the voices of the witches of *Macbeth* screeching "hubble, bubble, toil and trouble" around me. The light faded fast, and my fingers froze to my pencil as I frantically sketched as much as I could before darkness enveloped the scene. I wanted to ensure that the raw, bone-numbing cold emerged in my final painting. As I prepared to leave the Snout, little did I realise how much real 'toil and trouble' lay ahead. To get there, we had trekked through waist deep snow, Ron being driven on by the sheer excitement of anticipation. On reflection, we had left caution to the wind. Blizzards had swept across the moor, and we suddenly realised we were trapped with apparently no way out. Surrounded by a wall of snow and snow-filled cliffs and gullies, I was scared. But Ron, an experienced climber who I would trust with my life, spotted a loca-

tion: a cornice which overhung by about three feet (it's on the right hand side of my painting). We climbed on to it, then Ron, like a mole digging a tunnel, ploughed his way through the snow up and out of the Snout, shouting for me to follow. Drained of strength, I finally reached the top, thinking we would be home and dry. To my dismay and astonishment, swirling snow stretched for miles across the bleak land from one plateau to the next; our journey home had only just begun. We struggled against the drifts and biting wind until we reached a hut at the end of the reservoir where we sheltered for the night. Waking to a beautiful, crisp, bright morning, it was hard to believe just how forbidding the same moor had been some hours earlier. As I have said, you can never take nature for granted, her mood can change within seconds and she has the capacity to hold your life in her balance. I executed this painting immediately on my return home for I wanted to articulate all my emotions. I wanted to be able to hear the shrill echoes of the witches, feel the biting and numbing cold, smell the cutting clear air and know that this was one experience that I do not ever want to repeat.

42

Kilnsey

I feel compelled to include this study of Kilnsey Crag, the majestic lion's head that overlooks Wharfedale, for whenever I look at this unusual view with the lake and trout farm in the foreground, I realise I am not the only person who can enjoy and appreciate solitude and be at one with our environment. The many climbers who have scaled the overhang are equally at one with the elements and nature. Looking across to Kilnsey Crag encourages further comparison with my feelings and attitudes to my art and solitude. The climber must plan three moves ahead before he makes his next move. The same applies in watercolour painting; I need to think three strokes ahead, for like the climber, one false move can spell disaster. Unlike oil painting where an error may be covered once the paint is dry, no such safety net exists with watercolour. Once you have made a mistake you might as well tear up the paper. Achievement comes through planning your moves. Anne and I have always believed in the words of Manny Shinwell, "Be master of your own ship". That is why I have always believed that when people say to me that I'm lucky to be an artist, making a living from my love, my vocation, I always answer, "The only luck one has in your life is your health – the rest you make for yourself." Kilnsey Crag represents to me the epitome of what a man can achieve when taken to the limits; it encapsulates the strength and magnitude of the county and its people and is fully worthy of inclusion in this collection.

On a final note, the lion's head at Kilnsey is one of my favourite sculptures of all time, sculptured from stone by Mother Nature herself. I also believe that it is not by chance that the lion, who is the emblem of Great Britain, shows her head so magnificently in the heart of Yorkshire.

43

Snow in Maythorne Lane – looking to the Victoria

I was taken by the strange, dark drama of this scene of heavy snow surrounding Victoria Moor and Maythorne Lane. Storm clouds were rapidly crossing from the east, yet the winds which had bent and sculptured the trees were usually from the west. The elements appeared to be at war above Maythorne Farm, whose roof was illuminated against the sky. This sense of elemental conflict seized my imagination. I imagined that the clumps of grass protruding through the snow in the foreground were giant footprints (they also provided an ideal foreground to draw the viewer in) and I loved the cool indigo light shining on the scene. As I worked on my sketches with the wind swirling around, I knew I was in communion with my moor. In the icy cold, I scribbled these notes which summarise the whole essence of the painting and my drive as an artist:

There is nothing better than an ice cold day on the moor, when the snow is crisp-lying, the snow goes crunch under your boots and your face feels the sharpness of the clean winter air. I do believe that heaven and hell is on this earth we live in, and I feel a very lucky man to see this heaven.

44

Christmas morning – Victoria

This painting was conceived the morning after snow fell on Maythorne Lane: my intention was to portray the calm after the storm. When I left the farm the previous night, heavy flakes were already falling and by the time I reached home they were coming in fast flurries. I looked out of my bedroom that night in keen anticipation of the next day. On waking, I drove straight to Maythorne Farm. It never ceases to astonish me how the atmosphere of a place can change within a few hours and, as I got out of the car, I felt an immediate change. The turbulence had given way to calm. I relished being able to witness the warm light touching the snow-covered fields and the sun shining on buildings which had previously been hidden. What a difference a night can make. Everything was clear, fresh and settled after what must have been a terrifying snowstorm. What now attracted me to this scene were its details: snow clinging to the drystone walls like soft meringue, tree branches silhouetted like lace against the wintry sky – and the birds hovering in the daylight sun. Having survived the storm, they had to find food. Their quiet message was that life continues, no matter what the elements conspire to bring. We live to fight another day. The electricity and telegraph poles standing majestically upright took me back to 1970 and words that I had written comparing my inner feelings to these poles.

We are like the pole on the moor
We might bend with the wind and
Be a yes man – or stand to the wind
And hold hard to be ourselves.
But even then we might break.
ASHLEY JACKSON 1970

Footprints in the snow showed where the farmer had struggled in the night to bring his sheep in for shelter and food. It is on days like this that I can stand alone, inhale the intoxicating, crisp air and feel like the richest man on earth.

45

Ill wind – Fylingdales

Having lived through the 1960s and 1970s under the nuclear threat, I felt compelled to add this painting to the collection. The giant 'golf balls' at Fylingdales shadowed the movement of everyone's lives, whether we liked it or not. These early warning detectors represented a world that was out of our hands and in the control of politicians. Although they were being erected for our security, I can remember thinking that my life had never felt so fragile or vulnerable. I first set eyes on these monumental sculptures on the morning of what would prove to be a profoundly dark day: November 22, 1963 – JFK's assassination. I was taking part in the Lyke Wake Walk and, while treading the moor, the words of the dirge came as an echo: "Beware the Lyke Wake Walk, my son. . ." And yet it wasn't the moor that I was wary of, but the vast white domes on the horizon, reminders that we were all pawns in a political game of cat and mouse. I was desperate to catch the unabridged power and strength of this panorama. Yet for all its underlying menace, sheep were grazing peacefully in the foreground, symbols of life's continuity. The beautiful, rolling middle distance of the painting with its enchanting light embodied no man's land, a place of uncertainty over which the 'golf balls' cast a veil of confusion. The 'golf balls' silhouetted against the turbulent skyline can also hold the interpretation that life could end at the press of a political button. The essence of the painting concerns the futility of war and it takes me back to a poem I wrote in

1967 in memory of my father, a man who laid down his life so that I could paint freely.

Wars are hopeless,
For we fight the enemy
Only to make friends with them
When we could have been friends
All the while.
But, being what we are,
We fall out with friends
To make our enemies.
If only we could think
A bit more
For you know,
You are a long time dead.
I've a Japanese camera
When I could have had you – Dad.

FROM SKETCHBOOK 1967

46

Ribblehead – Man working at one with Nature

Whenever I look at this, I am filled with sadness. If only Beeching had not been so short-sighted in closing so many of the rail tracks that ran like veins across this country, killing off communities in the process. How badly they are needed and missed today. It is remarkable to think that the line over the Ribblehead Viaduct, once an artery in the network, now hosts only a local service, the Settle and Carlisle Railway. This painting represents a tribute to all that man has built with his hand, working in harmony with nature. An eminent American lawyer, Louis Nizer, once wrote, "A man who works with his hands is a labourer; a man who works with his hands and his brain is a craftsman, but a man who works with his hands and his brain and his heart is an artist."

47

Paths across the Pennines

I love walking the moors – the famous Lyke Wake Walk was one achievement of my youth. I have also traversed many miles of the Pennine Way which runs along the backbone of England. One of my favourite sections lies just above Holmfirth and is reached by taking the A635 out of Holmfirth past Wessenden Head on to a wonderful moorland highway which makes you feel as though you are on a roller coaster as it follows the swells and dips of the moor. You will eventually come to a rough parking area on your right where often stands the famous "Snoopy's Caravan" awaiting walkers, travellers – even painters – with freshly brewed tea and hot bacon sandwiches. From here, the route to the left goes to Black Hill and on to Holme Moss. I like to go this way occasionally and then from the Moss make my way down to Holme for lunch at the Fleece, where the landlord is usually waiting with a smile and friendly words of abuse! I then head towards Digley and back up on to the A635 to complete the few miles left to my car. This is quite a long walk but exhilarating. I chose on this particular day to turn right off the roadside where wooden palings are laid as a track on the moor to guard against erosion. This part of the moor is known as White Moss and the track leads to Black Moss Reservoir above Wessenden and eventually on to the main A62. It was, in fact, the palings that drew me to capture this location. To some people they appear ugly – but nature has a rare capacity to beautify the seemingly ugly. One only has to consider the Fylingdale 'golf balls'. Over time, nature had claimed them for herself and helped to soften their brash appearance, so that latterly they blended with the landscape to become a feature, not as HRH Prince of Wales would say, a "carbuncle". Nature had wrought a similar effect on the palings, softening and embracing them. They suggested to me a Jacob's Ladder, offering a light and pathway across a hostile moor. It is up on this moor that you will experience the sensation of being on the roof of the world; all your cares and thoughts will be blown away, and you will come away feeling that your whole body, mind and soul have been freshened and revived. The views are a match for any in the world. To sit there, as I often do with my rucksack and sandwiches, just listening to the song of a skylark or watching the grouse, is a joy beyond compare. With this painting, my desire was to convey the feeling that although the moor may look lonely, nature offers much for company: the sheep, the grouse, the skylark and the natural songs and rhythms of the moor. I had to smile as I put in my final details of the painting, the two telegraph poles that led to nowhere, and the fragmented drystone wall. As I added my own signature to my painting, so had the drystone waller left his signature on his work too, for the dry stone walls are an everlasting mark by mankind on our moorland, and we should be proud of them.

48

Castle Hill and Cartworth Moor

The wonderful cottages clinging to the slopes of the moor had so intrigued me in the spring of 1984 that I felt compelled to revisit the location and paint a similar view from an autumnal perspective. I set off for the site as dusk was falling, climbing the steep, narrow road called Rotcher from the centre of Holmfirth, passing a little hamlet called Dam House. I love it when I reach this part, for the moor starts to open and the claustrophobic feeling one can sometimes experience when surrounded by the clustered houses below soon disappears. Passing a row of weavers' cottages with what I call the 'gaffer's house' at the end – spacious and impressive – I realise just how much history is steeped in an area that was important to the Luddites during the Industrial Revolution. Further down the road, I reach the little knot of houses that I had captured earlier. This time, however, I climb over the wall to give the composition a different aspect, still keeping in view one of Huddersfield's most famous landmarks, Castle Hill. Its dominating tower, built to mark Queen Victoria's diamond jubilee, can be seen from many directions on the approach to Huddersfield. Whenever I have been away, and see this sight, I know I am nearly home. It is a great feeling. Having clambered over the wall, I was not disappointed by the view – the chimney pots standing rigid like chess men on the slate roofs of the white-washed cottages. I endeavoured to recreate the spirit and tone of the walls. Even the grime and dirt, marks of their sturdiness against the elements, enhanced the character of the buildings, enchanting me further. The tone, as I hope one can see, was still subtle, the trees helping to soften the view. To the right of my painting is a quarry where people once worked from dawn to dusk, labouring in all weathers to earn their living, emphasising to me how very fortunate I am to be able to pursue my vocation, my life as an artist.

I appreciate that many people are daunted by the thought of visiting the market town of Holmfirth, made famous by BBC's *The Last of the Summer Wine*. Folk are deterred for fear of being stuck with all the day-trippers in pursuit of their heroes. I make a special effort to tell people that Holmfirth and the surrounding area is not just about *Summer Wine* – it is a gem set in the heart of the Pennines. Peaceful, quiet locations can still be found within a two-minute drive of the town where you will be able to appreciate why not only did the BBC fall in love with the area, but I chose to make my home here. The next few paintings are my homage to this jewel of the Pennines.

49

Winter in the heart of Yorkshire

I include this painting of a snow-covered Cartworth Moor – completed some 10 years after my first attempt to depict this enchanting location – as it embodies my love for the natural beauty of the Holme Valley. No matter how long I live among its hills, I could never become bored. Yet I will never wholly know this place – no matter how hard I strive to fathom all her moods. Her character is forever changing. As these paintings show, she adopts a different dress and persona for each season, each containing the qualities that make her so enthralling and individual. Some people may find it hard to comprehend how I can compare my moors to a woman. But having known my wife, Anne, for some 45 years and these moors for a similar number, I feel justified in making the parallel, since I love them both passionately.

When I set out on this exhilarating, frosty November day in 1994, it was merely to enjoy a stroll. Snow had fallen three days previously, but low temperatures had kept it from cascading from the cottage roofs, even though their occupants would have kept the fires burning well into the early hours. Graceful icicles hung from gutterings and the frosted wall tops sparkled like a sugar-crusted meringue, glistening in the light. Castle Hill stood proud in the misty distance. How could one not be charmed by this scene? I was spellbound. Happily my brushes were in my rucksack and I secured in watercolour this delightful and alluring scene.

50

Underbank Old Road, Holmfirth

While I was still living in Barnsley as a boy, not seeing much of my beloved moors, Malcolm Haigh, a relation and friend, came to spend the weekend. We planned a cycle expedition which took us through Silkstone and Penistone and we eventually approached the steepled heights of Holme Moss from the Manchester side. Giving silent thanks for our Sturmey Archer gears, we arrived at the BBC transmitter and feasted our eyes on the view. There was the Holme Valley snaking into the far distance. What a beautiful sight! I still remember it with crystal clarity. Something told me that one day I would live here – as, indeed, I have for more than 30 years. *Underbank Old Road* is a must for inclusion in my selection of 60 paintings. It had just rained and the Yorkshire stone glistened. As there was no traffic about, I could set up my easel to capture telegraph wires that appeared to dance around a maypole in the wind. The education department of Barnsley Metropolitan Borough Council purchased this painting and I am pleased it went to a good home, as I really enjoyed creating it with vigorous strokes. I dedicated it to a true friend, Malcolm Haigh.

51

Holmfirth from Cartworth Moor

I created this painting in 1984 at a time when I found my style to be changing. Until then I had been using predominantly dark tones and the overall effect was of extreme tonal contrast, as can be seen clearly in *Underbank Old Road*. From this point, however, I found the skill to blend my tones more softly – something I had been striving years to attain. At last, at the age of 44, I felt that I was starting to achieve the effect I desired. It marked a personal breakthrough, and it is for this reason that I have such fondness for this painting. Atmosphere is so hard to capture. You can feel it all around you, but it is another matter to try and recreate its subtleties on paper and to communicate them strongly. So 1984 marked the beginning of my being able to reach this goal. Even now, though, some 15 years on, I do not succeed every time; I continue to strive for perfection, and believe I always will. For every painting that hangs on my gallery wall, at least seven will have been destroyed; you are only as good as your last work. I have often returned from a day on the moors, where I have braved all that the elements could muster, with just a few pieces of torn up paper. I do not get despondent at such times, however; I never regard it as wasting my time. If a painting does not come off, I tell myself I have been practising – and when it does, I have created a painting! Life is too short to worry about the odd failure.

52

Winter Solitude

Many people have asked over the years if I don't experience loneliness while out painting on barren, windswept moorland. My answer is that one can be lonely sitting among a hundred other people at the hub of a bustling city where no one is aware of your existence. That to me is loneliness. But to stand alone on the moors, with my paints and paper, surrounded by the sheer beauty of nature, that is solitude – and there is a huge difference. As an artist, I find it a privilege to experience solitude; to be at one with nature. In solitude, you never want the moment to pass, you want to distil and savour it. *Winter Solitude*, captured on an isolated moorland above Holmfirth, represented one such moment. Snow had fallen heavily the previous night, and I awoke to a crisp, white blanket spread across the valley. I set off to drive to one of my favourite locations, the Isle of Skye – a former pub, now a ruin – but had to abandon my car some miles from my destination and trek with my paints and the easel, bent against the biting wind. The snow crunched under my feet, I felt the brush of the Ice Maiden's breath on my skin, and the frost on my eyelids. Eventually, deep drifts made it almost impossible to continue; the only way forward was to walk along the wall tops. Just as I began to doubt whether I would reach my destination, I was met by a glowing halo of light, touching the moor and stopping me in my tracks. The scene before me was humbling, reinforcing man's insignificance against the elements. The light seemed to be highlighting all of nature's work from the previous night. Vegetation, wildlife and roads had been lost to the snow, the only visible man-made object was the drystone wall. As I rapidly sketched this scene, I became aware that the ghostly outline of the wall was in the shape of a question mark – was nature mocking me? I began to wonder, for solitude forces the artist to think deeply about life's meaning and purpose. At that moment, a sparrowhawk swooped down, desperate for food. My question was answered. Life is about survival; it is about striving to overcome the forces and obstacles nature places in its way. With this thought, I submerged myself in this morning scene. I have always said that to paint an apparently empty landscape is very difficult; all you have for support is nature's light, reflecting and shaping it. A view such as this cannot be seen literally, as truly there is nothing to see. But, to view it through your spiritual, all-seeing eye, allows the moor to come alive. The strong and soft tones seize the opportunity to appear and show themselves in their true glory. I have tried throughout my life to capture the spirit of moors, an experience which often leaves me humbled yet exhilarated – none more so than here. Nature humbled me with her pure strength, power and light, yet allowed me to exult in her glow. How can one not truly enjoy solitude?

53

Frozen stiff at Wagstaffes

I have a fascination for the potent image and rich symbolism of isolated farmhouses on snow-covered moors. I was frozen stiff when I arrived at Wagstaffes Farm, high in the Pennines. The sky was threatening to unload more snow, holding it like a child with a water balloon, eager to burst it. It always amazes me that a brooding, near-black sky can produce such pure brilliant white covering. I love to see the sky in motion – the storm was beginning to surround me – and its movement lent a special excitement. The barbed wire was whistling eerily in the wind – providing a wondrous background as the storm approached its crescendo. Wagstaffes Farm may look empty and isolated but the sudden lurching of an Alsatian on its chain is sufficient reminder that it is used and lived in! On the day the chain breaks, I often wonder who will be more surprised, the dog or me! The farm is situated very close to Flowery Fields near Hade Edge, above Holmfirth. When I came to live in Holmfirth some 30 years ago I was told that I had to learn the words of the Holmfirth anthem – *Pratty Flowers* – before I could imagine living in the area. Pratty, by the way, means pretty. Looking at this painting, it is hard to believe that when the snow disappears, this land is home to many species of moorland flower. This abundance was the inspiration for the anthem, which is sung – and has been for many generations – with pride at local functions.

Abroad for pleasure as I was a-walking
It was one summer's, summer's evening clear
There I beheld a most beautiful damsel, lamenting
for her shepherd dear.

The dearest evening that e'er I beheld thee
Ever, evermore with the lad I adore;
Wilt thou go fight yon French and Spaniards?
Wilt thou leave me thus, my dear.

No more to yon green banks will I take thee
With pleasure for to rest thyself and view the lambs.
But I will take thee to yon green gardens
Where the pratty flowers grow,
Where the pratty, pratty flowers grow.

This painting I dedicate to the people of the Holme Valley who have allowed me to share their awe-inspiring, beautiful terrain – a land that I cherish.

THE COLLECTION   127

54

Isolation

This painting typifies a winter afternoon high in the Pennines, the soft moor struggling to radiate light and warmth through the dim, cheerless air. When I captured Mrs Sanderson's Farm high upon Digley Moor, I wanted to convey the feeling of being caught in a swell on a foaming, tempestuous, icy sea, with the moorland farm pitched high upon it. I was anxious to convey the freezing temperature of the afternoon, a cold that pierced to the very bones. Whenever I study this painting – the snow clinging to the slates, frost like torn and tattered lace on the fence, gaunt trees sculpted by the winds; even in death, the mountain ash, bleached skeletal white, still stands monumentally against all that the elements throw at it – my imagination allows me to roll back the years. In spite of the fierce cold, I can recall the joy in knowing that there was life within those walls. Often when painting, I feel a warmth inside me. I am filled with an excitement that stirs and quickens the spirit, like first love. Sheer concentration holds and fuels that feeling, yet the moment my work is complete, it is as though I am brought straight to my senses. It is then I feel the atmosphere of the day. As I finally signed my name to the painting, a desire for physical warmth took over, and I knocked upon the door to be welcomed with true Yorkshire hospitality into the security of Mrs Sanderson's farm.

55

Home for Christmas

"The sky is the drama of your painting. You must see this drama, feel the wind on your face and smell the scent of the moor. If you can smell it, you will paint it." I wrote these words in a sketchbook in 1972 and they encapsulate my feelings for this work. The drama of the sky stopped me in my tracks. It was not an ideal time: I was desperately trying to get home over the tops from Manchester, having been to buy my wife a Christmas gift. As I made my way down to the village of Holme, the quality of the sky forced me to stop. Even though another snowstorm was looming, the light dimming and the temperature dropping, I felt impelled to record this scene in my sketchbook. I parked the car as best I could and crossed over the wall on to the foreground field to get the best composition, ensuring that I absorbed all the power, strength and brooding atmosphere swirling around me. As I sketched, a car passed by – then stopped. Its driver cautiously walked up and half whispered, half cried, "Is that you Ashley?" The driver was Wilbert Kemp, a local amateur artist and hairdresser who I knew quite well. He had feared that nature had finally claimed me and that I had taken my final breath while out capturing the Yorkshire I love so well. I always smile when I look at this painting, for although I frightened poor Wilbert, I would not be afraid to die in such a way. Indeed, I can think of no better way to leave this earth than to succumb to the elements that I have striven so long to depict.

56

White Plains – Boshaw

I rarely paint to commission, preferring to paint to please myself. When, however, your eldest daughter – who is due to be married – looks you in the eye and says that for a wedding gift "I would like a painting of the building that will become my new home", how can a father refuse? I was humbled by this request and eager to make this my best work to date. Although I was eager for perfection, I anticipated a long struggle – not least because I was, on this occasion, going against my beliefs. I have always maintained that you cannot plan to paint a good painting any more than you can plan to fall in love. Heather, like me, is passionate about the moors and spends many an hour running the fells and walking its heaths, so the barn house that she and her fiancé, Charles, purchased high on the hills above Holmfirth, overlooking Boshaw Reservoir, came as no surprise. It stood solid against the prevailing winds, looking out across the moors. This was to be her dream home. Many people could not appreciate why she loved it so much, but I knew – hence my desire to portray it. Like me, Heather loves the solitude and isolation that snow brings and I decided to paint it when the first heavy fall came. Perhaps it was the pressure I had imposed on myself to produce an exceptional work, but I tore up my first effort. Dissatisfied with myself, I went home despondent and irritable. My wife, sensing my disappointment, took out some notes that I had made about my love of painting which I had written when Anne was pregnant with

Heather in 1967. In them I had likened painting to a drug:

I go mad every time a painting is complete,
I have never been satisfied with any of my work,
Lord knows why people want to buy my work.
Painting has become a drug to me, and like
Drugs, it has side effects that not everyone
Sees, but my wife.

They must have had some effect for, a few weeks later when heavy snows again fell, I went up to Boshaw, this time with a different attitude. If it came off I had done a painting for Heather; if it didn't, I had been practising – I had nothing to lose. The scene could not have been more perfect. The barn house stood in deep, drifting snow on the ridge, silhouetted supremely on the skyline by the menacing and swirling sky. As I put my first brush stroke on to my paper intuition told that this was going to work. I also knew that although some people might find this painting cold, bleak, intimidating and almost too powerful to live with, Heather would love it. On presenting her with the finished work, her face and eyes said it all – it was the hardest piece I have ever had to paint, but it was worth it, her pride in her old dad shone through. Today, it hangs in its full glory in her home.

57

Christmas high above Castle Hill

"Too Long a Winter" are the words that resonate in my mind as I view this painting. It embodies the harsh reality of winter high in the Pennines: a winter where the snow lasts long after it has fallen, hardened by biting, whipping winds. Even the sheep have to retreat to the haven of the farm. It is when you reflect upon such a landscape that you fully appreciate the grit of those who strive to earn their living from these moors; life is never easy for them. This scene lies on the borders of Barnsley, a town once noted more for its slag heaps than its natural beauty. For years it was the butt of music hall jokes, but the image of popular prejudice no longer holds. The borough is surrounded by wonderful countryside and is home to great, strong and characterful folk. The actor Brian Glover, whom I was proud to call a friend, came from Barnsley. As I looked out across this vista, and saw the kestrel in flight high above me, my thoughts were with him. Now, at last, his spirit was free to fly across God's Yorkshire; to absorb the liberty that only death brings. I dedicated this painting to Brian – God bless.

58

Winter at Heather's

This painting features the unadopted lane that ran to Heather's barn, captured in the painting *White Plains – Boshaw*. When-ever I drove to visit Heather and Charles along this typical West Riding dirt track, the aspect that fascinated me was the concrete street light that leaned precariously. It intrigued me and became the inspiration of the painting. When Heather and Charles first bought the barn house, I almost envied their finding the strength of character to purchase a home in so untamed a setting, which to me was the epitome of paradise. I had often dreamed of having a farm high on the Pennines, with magnificent views from every window. But, remember, this is a place where the wind strips you of your breath; where you perpetually walk bent over against the wind; where winter seems to last for six months, and where, come the heavy snow, you are beyond reach of any amenity. This is also a place where in summer you need to carry your own windbreak, even on a sunny day; where the weather is two coats colder than down in the valley; and where crocuses and daffodils go down on their knees praying you won't plant them there! And yet it is so beautiful and alluring that I can understand why my daughter loves it so. But although I love being out on wild, cold and desolate days, there is nothing nicer than being able to return to the warmth of your home, or the serenity of the garden, where you can sit out without a sheet of corrugated roof shield-ing you from the wind. It takes a hardy character to live out

generations in the same place. Perhaps I am turning into an old softy, for much as I love to paint the wild moors, I admit that I appreciate being able to return to the comfort of my home and, with a glass of fine Scotch whisky in my hand, relax by a glow-ing fire and admire my work hung on the wall – the end to a perfect day.

59

Frosty morning

The aroma of sweet salty bacon frying and the smoke idly drifting from the chimney in the early morning air drew me to this scene. A heavenly quiet surrounded me, even the bird flying low in the sky seemed suspended. The moment was transfixed, dangling in the ambience of the crisp morning and I too was frozen by the scene. I had not been early enough to make the first tracks in the virgin snow, an act since childhood that still gives me much pleasure, but this did not deter from the moment. I was heading along the road to one of my favourite sights, one which when I scan across its panorama makes me feel like a millionaire. I view all of God's county lying magnificently before me from the windmills on Ogden Moor, glistening in the distant light, to Ferrybridge; the vista is unbelievable. This day, though, my legs were not going to take me any further until I captured the beautiful scene. As the mist lay still and low, hiding the distant hills, my heart and soul were intent on capturing the sentiment of this crisp winter's day. I truly felt at ease with this painting, everything came together, although I would have loved to have joined the family inside, to eat with them their hearty breakfast and drink with them a pot of scalding tea. The scene had such intensity and power that as I painted, the warmth I felt from within was more than enough for me to endure the frost biting at my fingers. My morning finished exquisitely with an enthralling moment stood on my hill, drinking in the light, absorbing the intoxicat-

ing, spectacular and magnificent snow-blanketed panorama that I had set out initially to view. A precious and treasured day to keep within my mind and soul for ever. Looking at this painting again is like opening Pandora's Box; all my senses that morning come alive and I relive the moment. How lucky I am to be alive and healthy on a day such as this.

60

Ewden Valley 1963

Of all my paintings, this without doubt is my most precious and priceless. I owe everything to this study of a cottage in the Ewden Valley; it cannot command a higher place of honour in my life. Were I to choose the painting from this collection that holds the most sentiment and influence, it would be this. It began as a raw watercolour sketch and I can remember being intrigued by the whole atmosphere that hung around it. As time passed I progressed from art school to a commercial art studio, then as a romantic newly-wed I dug it out from my old pad. In a tribute to those days of innocence – and to mark our first wedding anniversary – I painted the cottage which we had first visited as teenagers, to give to Anne. I took the finished work to the little art shop in Church Street, Barnsley (which I now own), to have it framed. Miss Haden, a former art teacher who ran the shop, could not believe that I had painted this water-colour. She asked me if I would bring it the following week to Barnsley Art Society's critique night. As a non-member I had to keep quiet and let her place it among the other works to be viewed by these out-of-town critics. All the names on the works were taped over to guard against favouritism. Much to my surprise, but not Miss Haden's, three paintings out of the 70 entered were chosen for appraisal, among them mine. I was astonished by the glowing report; words like 'soul', 'technique' and 'inner-feeling' were mentioned. I was dazed to believe they were talking about my own work. When they drew back the tape and asked who had painted it, it was an embarrassed 22 year old who stood up to acknowledge the praise. The critics, unaware I was a non-member, asked questions and I told them I had loved watercolour painting all my life. I cannot begin to tell you, having led a young life with no encouragement or support from my family, how much it meant to me hearing men and women I had never set eyes on before speaking so highly of my work. With Miss Haden by my side, who had risked getting herself into hot water amongst the art society for bringing me along, this gave me an inner confidence that I had never felt before. The event was a major turning point; I shudder to think how differently my life would have turned out had it not been for that evening. I would probably be still working as a sign-writer. My wife, being a true Yorkshire lass, knew that if times were hard I would – even though it was an anniversary gift – sell the painting to keep the wolf from the door. So, without more ado, she bought it from her savings for £10 – an incredible amount of money, the most I had been given for painting. But Anne knew that to give me its retail worth would emphasise her confidence in me and fuel my ambition and drive. As an unknown, newly-wed artist with no finance and no name it was not easy. I owe all of what I have achieved to Anne who has stood by me and covered my back when there was no wall behind me. As you can guess the painting of Ewden Valley has remained with us ever since and hangs proudly in our home.

Appendix

One Man Exhibitions

1963 Brighouse
1964 Newark Art Gallery, Nottingham
1966 Crows Nest Gallery, Dewsbury
1967 Brighouse Art Gallery
1968 Wakefield Art Gallery
1968 Cannon Hall Gallery, Barnsley
1969 Upper Grosvenor Gallery, West End, London
1974 The Mall Gallery, FBA, London
1977 Municipal Gallery, Valencia, Spain
1978 Kidderminster Art Gallery
1979 Maclaurin Gallery, Glasgow, Scotland
1979 Foyles Gallery, Charing Cross Road, London
1983 The Old Barn, Ruislip
1984 Milan
1984 Washington, USA
1985 Dallas, USA
1985 New York, USA
1985 Chicago, USA
1986 Milan
1986 The Mall Gallery, FBA, West End, London, "Ashley Jackson's Vision of Turner" – Sponsored by the Yorkshire Post.
1987 Cooper Art Gallery, Barnsley
1987 San Francisco, USA
1987 "Ashley Jackson's Vision of Turner". Opened by HRH Prince of Wales – Sponsored by Bass.
1988 New York, USA
1989 St Louis, USA

1990 Huddersfield Art Gallery "My Way, Art to the People" – retrospective exhibition – Sponsored by Yorkshire TV.
1991 Lauron Gallery, Ilkley – "In Mood with the Moor".
1991 John Worthy Gallery, Leek – "In Harmony with the Moor".
1992 The Coach House Gallery, Lincoln
1993 United Society of Artists, London
1993 Patchings Art Gallery, Nottingham
1994 Yorkshire Post HQ, Leeds
1994 Rotherham Art Gallery – "My Mistress and I – The Yorkshire Moors".
1995 Cooper Art Gallery, Barnsley – "Here's to you, Dad" – touring exhibition – Smith Gallery, Brighouse, Dewsbury Town Hall, Doncaster Art Gallery
1996 "From Yorkshire with Love" – Beningbrough Hall, York, Wakefield Art Gallery, Sewerby Hall, Bridlington
1997 "Earth, Wind and Fire", Salford Art Gallery
1999 "Twilight of the Twentieth Century", Cartwright Hall, Bradford
2000 "Dawns a New Day", Royal Armouries, Leeds

Group Shows/Mixed Exhibitions

Royal Watercolour Society, Open Exhibition, London
Royal Institute of Painters in Watercolour, Open Exhibition, London
Britain in Watercolour, Federation of British Artists, Open Exhibition – work was chosen for touring exhibition.
Harrogate Art Gallery – Yorkshire Watercolour Society
House of Commons
Lowry Gallery, Salford, Manchester, Mixed exhibition with sculptor Sam Tonkis

1974 Guest exhibitor by invitation in exhibition featuring Picasso, Dali and Miro.
United Society of Artists, London
1995 (and 1996) Beverley Minster Fine Art Exhibition

Television Productions
1968 Omnibus Programme, BBC
1978 (and 1985) Own television series of Pebble Mill at One, BBC
1981 "Once in a Lifetime – My own Flesh and Blood" – Documentary on Ashley Jackson, ITV
1982 "Making the Most of...."
1984 (to 1988) "Ashley Jackson's World of Art", three six-part series on PBS TV USA
1990 BBC Look North, "Profile of an Artist"
1990 "A Brush with Ashley", his own series on Yorkshire TV
1992 May, "A Brush with Ashley, II", Yorkshire TV and Satellite
1993 "A Brush with Ashley" III
1990 (to 1996) Satellite TV, The Learning Channel – "A Brush with Ashley"
1994 Wire TV – Mini Series
1995 "A Brush with Ashley" IV
1997 "A Brush with Ashley" V
1998 "A Brush with Ashley" VI
1999 "A Brush with Ashley" VII
2000 "A Brush with Ashley" VIII
 "Ashley Jackson's Yorkshire" Yorkshire TV

Books Published
1981 "My Brush with Fortune" – Secker and Warburg
 An Artist's Notebook
 "Ashley Jackson's World of Art", Volumes 1, 2, and 3, – Alexandra Art Corporation, USA.
1992 "Painting in the Open Air" – Harper Collins
1993 "A Brush with Ashley" – Box Tree Publications
1994 "Painting the British Isles – a Watercolourist's Journey" – Box Tree Publications

Entries
"Who's Who in Art"
"Debretts, People of Today"

Honours
1996 Ashley was a former student of Barnsley School of Art, and in his honour they established the "Ashley Jackson Gallery" on their site at Barnsley College, housing 26 originals by Ashley. The gallery is open to the public, Fridays 3.30-5pm.
1996 The Yorkshire Awards for Art and Entertainment

Ashley Jackson Galleries 13/15 Huddersfield Road, Holmfirth, Huddersfield HD7 1JR. Website: ashley-jackson.co.uk